Drawn and Dangerous

SIMONE CASTALDI

Drawn and Dangerous
ITALIAN COMICS OF THE 1970S AND 1980S

UNIVERSITY PRESS OF MISSISSIPPI / JACKSON

www.upress.state.ms.us

The University Press of Mississippi is a member
of the Association of American University Presses.

First printing 2010

∞

Library of Congress Cataloging-in-Publication Data

Castaldi, Simone.
  Drawn and dangerous : Italian comics of the 1970s
and 1980s / Simone Castaldi.
      p. cm.
  Includes bibliographical references and index.
  ISBN 978-1-60473-749-3 (cloth : alk. paper) —
ISBN 978-1-60473-777-6 (ebook) 1. Comic books, strips,
etc.—Italy—History and criticism. I. Title.
  PN6765.C37 2010
  741.5'6945—dc22   2010013085

British Library Cataloging-in-Publication Data available

#60731976|

Contents

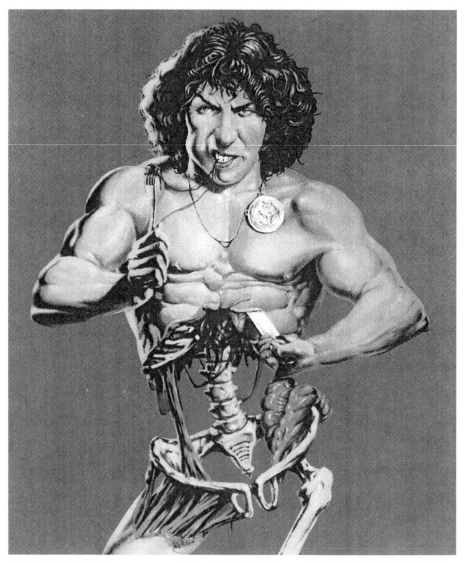

Liberatore, Tanino. Artwork for the cover of *Cannibale* n.8.

Preface

My first encounter with the comics discussed in this book occurred many years ago. It was 1978, I was ten years old. I walked past a newsstand, glanced at the comic book section, and froze in my tracks.

Among the dizzying mass of publications on display—newspapers, political weeklies, fashion and sports magazines, paperbacks, and even encyclopedias offered volume-by-volume every week—what attracted my attention was the cover of a magazine with an illustration of a skeleton. Actually, only the lower half was a skeleton. The upper part was still living flesh: a young man with long curly hair vigorously chewing— *something*. He brandished a fork in one hand as the other jabbed a knife in his own ribs. Between the upper and lower halves of his body, flesh gave way to bone revealing residual muscular fibers, a tract of intestine resting on the hipbone, and various scarlet filaments hanging obscenely from the rib cage.

The headline said *Cannibale* (cannibal), and what was left of the young man stared right at me.

Somehow in the midst of this strange feast, the most striking detail was the background color—liver red. As inconspicuous as a bikini-clad girl at a papal audience, the *thing* rested between issues of *Topolino* (Mickey Mouse in Italian) and *Tex* (a popular cowboy hero aimed at young adults). Captivated, yet unable to make up my mind, I just stood there for a while.

Then I decided to touch it.

The paper felt different—cheaper, yellower than other comics. But I didn't dare take it off the rack—"You take it off the rack, you bought it," was the unwritten rule of the vendors. What if I didn't like it? And what if there was *more* liver-colored art inside?

I gave up and bought a copy of *Linus*, a non-threatening adult comics monthly featuring a Charles M. Schulz Snoopy on the cover. No liver, no forks.

The following day, unable to think of anything other than that mysterious cannibal (Was he really eating himself? Why? And why was he looking at *me*?), I returned to the newsstand to purchase it.

But it was gone.

I eventually forgot about it until several years later when I learned that the authors of the new magazine *Frigidaire* had also been responsible for the now-defunct *Cannibale*.

The adult comics of the period connected me to the outside world: one not revealed by the news on the Italian national channels, nor the anesthetized press of the major newspapers of the time—and certainly not the Italian school system. I read about the El Salvador death squads (the authentic photo reportage of the massacres topped the fictional cover of *Cannibale*), the Mafia resurgence in southern Italy, baby pushers in American metropolises, time travelers, the slow deterioration of the USSR, William Burroughs discussing Scientology, the latest news on artificial foods, androids built with pieces of photocopy machines, etc. Truth *and* fiction were so much better than fictional truth.

So it is to these divulgators, and in particular those tied to the magazines *Cannibale* and *Frigidaire*, to which this effort is dedicated: Vincenzo Sparagna, Stefano Tamburini, Tanino Liberatore, Massimo Mattioli, and all the others.

In particular, I would like to dedicate this book to the memory of Andrea Pazienza, one of the most important as well as most celebrated practitioners of the comic art form, who many years ago hosted the author in his house in Bologna, graciously agreeing to an in-depth interview, excerpts of which are included here.

Finally, a particular note of gratitude goes to Filippo Scòzzari, comic artist extraordinaire and author of one of the most revealing and entertaining books on the end of the '70s period in Italy, *Prima pagare poi ricordare*. In addition to a lengthy interview, much of which is incorporated into the book, Scòzzari read the entire manuscript, providing invaluable input. For this, for having opened windows on unsuspected worlds—for having shocked me, informed me, and plainly making me laugh myself silly for almost thirty years—for Suor Dentona, la Mengoli, Capitan Dulciora, Primo Carnera, Towloose Lowtrack, Nekator Super Fly, and il Dottor Gek, I respectfully thank him.

Drawn and Dangerous

Introduction

In October 1977 the magazine *Alter*, at that time the most prestigious publication of adult comics in Italy, featured a fourteen-page story by Filippo Scòzzari titled "Un buon impiego" (A Good Position). Set in a not-too-distant future in and around the Italian city of Bologna, "Un buon impiego" told the story of Louigi (sic), an unemployed gay man who was preparing to kill the newly elected president and take his place.

In Scozzari's grotesque vision, Italy is a police state controlled by the Communist Party. On his way to the center of Bologna, Louigi passes several checkpoints, witnesses the killing of a political dissident by the party's militia, and is repeatedly taunted by police officers because of his homosexuality, all the while concealing the gun he intends to use on the President.

Having reached the square where the president is delivering his acceptance speech, Louigi takes advantage of the confusion generated by earlier assassination attempts (the first by a student protester, the second by a dissident intellectual), shoots the president and—in accordance with the law, takes his place. Compared to typical Italian adult comics of the time, "Un buon impiego" came out of nowhere and its uniqueness must have been immediately evident to readers.

Alter was the sister magazine of the venerable *Linus*, the first Italian comics magazine to publish stories geared to an adult readership. Until 1977 *Alter* had published reprints of celebrated American strips such as Chester Gould's *Dick Tracy*, occasional stories by cutting-edge French artists such as Reiser, Jean-Claude Forest, and Georges Pichard—and a generous serving of works by established Italian auteurs such as Hugo Pratt, Sergio Toppi, and Dino Battaglia.

The latter group's stories mostly dealt with the adventure genre, imbued with references to the nineteenth-century American and European novel. Most importantly, both *Linus* and *Alter* belonged to the milieu of left-wing culture dominating the Italian landscape since the post-war years, and their editorial policies were to some extent in line with the politics of the Italian Communist Party (PCI).

The appearance of Scòzzari's story in *Alter* showed that in 1977 things were changing fast—and not just in comics. Scòzzari's dystopian future was clearly a grotesque satire of the myths of communist revolution and the rising sun of socialism perpetrated by the Party's propaganda. What was not immediately evident to *Alter*'s readers accustomed to the political Manichaeism of the times, however, was the author's ideological orientation. He certainly did not belong to the conservative right (a non-affiliation guaranteed, if nothing else, by his appearance in the pages of *Alter*), nor to the Catholic center-right, which had governed the country for the past thirty years.

At the same time, his carnival-style satire of the Party, along with his irreverent portrayal of obtuse factory workers, cheering masses, senile Partisans, and the mocking references to Bologna's Communist mayor, Renato Zangheri, made his association with the left-wing environment equally unlikely. What's more, Bologna's Communist administration was often referenced by the Party as a shining example of socialism at work. Therefore, the question on many readers' minds was why the author specifically targeted Bologna, the best of all possible cities.

The answer was that Bologna had recently been the setting of one of the pivotal protests of the alternative left-wing Movement of '77 and had consequently become the stage for one of the most brutal episodes of police repression of the decade. The mobilization of tanks employed to quell the riots, with the authorization of the city's political administration, was conclusive proof to many that the official left no longer represented a viable alternative to the conservative Christian center-right. The roots of the student Movement of '77 and its political background will be discussed, but note that for the first time in the field of adult comics— and for the first time in the Italian cultural arena at large—a non-aligned voice was commenting on present-day events, in real time, by mixing fiction and journalism. Even more relevant was the fact that this voice sprang from a venue as unexpected as comics.

Besides the strictly political aspects of "Un buon impiego," other qualities set Scòzzari's story apart from earlier adult comics. For example, most Italian auteur comics belonged to the adventure genre, often as highbrow adaptations of literary classics (*The Arabian Nights*, *Moby Dick*, the short stories of Edgar Allan Poe and Guy de Maupassant), and the overall style of these comics was inspired by American comic art staples such as Milton Caniff (*Terry and the Pirates*, *Steve Canyon*) and the tradition of book illustrators such as Gustave Doré.

FIG. I.1 Scòzzari, Filippo. *Un buon impiego*. The grotesque tone of the narrative is established from the start through the use of extreme close-ups and slow zoom-outs in the opening sequence of the story.

Conversely, the style of "Un buon impiego" was visibly influenced by the aesthetics of the American underground comic artists of the late '60s and early '70s who were virtually unknown in Italy. While the majority of the old auteurs strove to achieve an elegant and pleasant line—a "clean" page, and a marked degree of realism—Scòzzari's art boasted grotesque effects, deformed anatomies, and an all-encompassing impression of filth that emanated from the brush line: enormous noses and genitalia, misshapen bellies, and an idiosyncratic abundance of body hair.

"Un buon impiego" displayed influences from Richard Corben and Greg Irons, veterans of the American underground comic movement, along with many elements derived from the groundbreaking work of Will Eisner (fig. I.1). On a diegetic level, another innovative element of Scòzzari's story was its gay hero. Homosexuality was certainly not an issue addressed by Italian comics at the time, even those geared toward an adult readership, but with "Un buon impiego," not only was a gay character featured—he was also the "positive" hero of the story. Moreover, breaking an unspoken taboo, our hero was shown having sex right at the opening of the narration.

Just as innovative and subversive was Scòzzari's strong intertextual leaning. Old-school auteur comics gravitated dangerously toward kitsch, maintaining a subordinate position in respect to their sources. The interplay of references worked mainly as a strategy to guarantee citizenship in the realm of the high arts. Scòzzari's story, however, being closer to the postmodern ethos of pastiche, quoted with an irreverent attitude toward cultural hierarchies: a painting by American artist Edward Hopper; the independent journal of the '77 Movement, *Zut*; a cut-and-paste photograph of activist, journalist, and media-pirate Bifo (Franco Berardi); infamous magistrate Bruno Catalanotti, who prosecuted many of the student activists of the Bologna movement; the science fiction of Philip K. Dick and Michael Moorcock. The poetics of "Un buon impiego" contained all the characteristics the new adult comics would develop more fully in the following years through the works of Andrea Pazienza, Tanino Liberatore, Massimo Mattioli, Stefano Tamburini, and many others. And it was not by chance that this new and vital strand of adult comics sprang up in the midst of the social and political upheaval of the Italian '77.

In the collective Italian consciousness, two years stand out in the final decades of the twentieth century: 1968 and 1977. The former, epitomized by the first wave of student protests, is remembered as a time of hopeful and constructive collective action: the utopian alliance between middle-class students and factory workers, the expansion of new productive political practices, the development of the feminist movement; whereas, the latter—coinciding with the rise of extreme left- and right-wing terrorism, violent student protests, political stagnation, a severe economic crisis—is avoided to the point that its cultural and political outcomes are often regarded as taboo.

Nonetheless, the late '70s and early '80s were a particularly lively time in Italy, both culturally and politically. The adult comics reflected and incorporated many of the novel issues these troubled times put on the table: the dawn of micro-politics, disillusionment with all-encompassing systems of thought, the rising debate of postmodernism, and the questioning of the divide between high and low cultural levels.

For nearly a decade, from the mid-'70s to the mid-'80s, Italian adult comics served as a neutral meeting ground, a vital link between popular art and the exponents of sanctioned cultural areas. Thanks to this unsuspected medium, painters, art critics, and literary authors exchanged experiences with comic creators, lending and borrowing ideas and approaches. One has only to flip through *Frigidaire*, the main publication of the new adult comics, to witness these connections in action: the call-and-response between comic book artists and painters such as Mario Schifano, intellectuals such as Achille Bonito Oliva, or contemporary composers such as Sylvano Bussotti.

Furthermore, these comics and their authors, as a central part of the counterculture of those years, were in the forefront of challenging not only the implicit division between highbrow and lowbrow culture, but also the long-lived cold war parochialism of the political and cultural debate in Italy. And, indeed, the most distinctive trait of the new adult comics is their sense of freedom, both aesthetically and ideologically, and their ravenous appetite for cultural appropriation, from Carl Barks' *Donald Duck* to the Russian Suprematist painters—often within the space of a single panel.

The title of the first magazine of the new adult comics, *Cannibale*, was therefore a very appropriate choice, as was the image that appeared on the cover of one of its earliest issues: the young man busy devouring himself with knife and fork, while staring intently at the reader. All the main coordinates of the new adult comics and the new cultural atmosphere emerging at the end of the '70s were put neatly on display: the voracious intertextuality, the postmodern meta-discursive strategy (the "cannibal" medium feeding on itself), the pop culture iconography, and a marked inclination toward a playful poetics of cruelty.

In a recent survey of Italian contemporary art of the last three decades, *Prima e dopo il 2000*, Renato Barilli, literary critic and veteran of the neo-avant-gardist group Gruppo '63, identified a pendulum shift in twentieth-century Italian art. On one extreme stands a movement toward conservation and aesthetic accumulation—on the other side, a forward-looking disruptive tendency. In broader terms, the forerunning evidence of such alternating movement can be traced, in modern times, in the shift from eighteenth-century neoclassicism and nineteenth-century romanticism.

In the twentieth century, however, these oscillations intensify. One example in Italian culture is the shift from the Futurist anti-cultural ethos and the movement of reappropriation epitomized by the paintings of Giorgio De Chirico, especially after the mid-'20s. However, by the mid-'70s, these two opposing movements appear to coincide. If in the '60s Italy had a *neo*-avant-garde, the late '70s proposed a *trans*-avant-garde, where the emphasis rested on transversality, rather than on the new.

The new adult comics embraced this condition with great ease and, as I will argue, represent one of the most accomplished examples of these two opposite drives simultaneously at work. In fact, the emergence of this notion in the new adult comics took place concurrently with the same aesthetic development in the field of the "high" visual arts, vastly outpacing similar outcomes in the field of literature. Mainly narrative, while at the same time highly self-referential in their structures—avant-gardist in their stances, but encyclopedic in their intertextual component—the adult comics represent a key element to the understanding of the Italian cultural debate between the '70s and '80s.

Given the nature of the subject at hand, my discussion necessarily unfolds along the lines of a marked interdisciplinary approach. The post-'77 adult comics thrived in a highly diverse cultural environment. The debate in the field of the visual "high" arts involving the appearance of artist groups such as the *nuovi-nuovi* and the painters of the trans-avant-garde, the sudden development of a multifaceted independent art-rock music scene, and the emergence of the new independent press and independent "free" radio stations were all instances of a climate within which the new adult comics entertained tight and fruitful exchanges.

Clearly, intertextuality was for the new comics not merely a symptom of the postmodern times they represented, but also a sign of the active interrelation between diverse cultural areas that marked the late '70s and early '80s in Italy. Although today this quality is endemic to the majority of current cultural products, it was then still perceived in conservative areas as a threat to the well-being of "culture" as an abstract concept.

Finally, the reason this study concentrates on the adult comics of the '70s and '80s is not only because comics production reached its peak in maturity, complexity, and wealth of discursive strategies during those years, but also because analysis of these comics offers the possibility for a fresh outlook on the cultural situation of the time. I argue that restoring this missing piece is a vital step toward a better understanding of an important and problematic decade in Italian socio-political history. By filling this particular slot in the context of the debate on the Italy of the late '70s and early '80s, this book intends to bring to light vital cultural connections and, in the end, to contribute to the reassessment of this *lost* decade.

CHAPTER ONE

Italian Adult Comics Before '77

The Italian comics of the late '70s and '80s belong to a particular niche of the medium of sequential art we identify here as "adult comics." The term "adult," rather than referring exclusively to content (although content represents an important discriminating factor) or to an aesthetic and arbitrary cultural evaluation, is employed here simply in reference to the postulated age-group that these works target and, consequently, to the specific competence of their implied readership.

It is true that a strict distinction between comics for young readers and those meant for adults is often problematic and indeed, many grey areas exist; one has only to consider the possible double readings offered by such comics as Walt Kelly's *Pogo*, George Herriman's *Krazy Kat*, or Lyonel Feininger's *Kin-der-Kids*. Nevertheless, the great majority of these works, their capacity to provide an engaging and satisfying aesthetic experience for adults notwithstanding, were marketed to young readers.

Curiously, for a medium traditionally regarded as entertainment for children and young adults—comics in its infancy were consumed indiscriminately by all age groups: from the pioneering work of Rodolphe Töpffer in the early 1800s to the Sunday newspaper supplements devised by William Randolph Hearst at the turn of the twentieth century. Comics became a literature exclusively for the young with their independence from the newspapers and the appearance of the first comic books around the mid-'30s.[1] This step in the evolution of the medium is extremely relevant, not only because it defined an exclusive age group as readership, but by placing comics below the radar of official popular culture, it laid the groundwork for the development of adult comics some three decades later. As Kirk Varnedoe and Adam Gopnik note:

> Comic strips, like the movies, were a public and ceremonial form. They were part of a larger experience of the newspaper, integrated into a ribbon of wars and sports and society. They had a place in a hierarchy. A comic book, on the other hand, was something you had to walk into a store and buy; it was in its very nature outside parental control. (. . .) The comic book presupposed, as a condition for its existence, the fragmentation of the genuinely mass or folk audience that had embraced the comic strip. (182)

Contrary to the development of the medium in America, comics appeared in Italy toward the end of the first decade of the twentieth century exclusively as children's entertainment. The most prestigious publication in these early stages was *Il Corriere dei Piccoli*, a separate weekly supplement to the venerable newspaper *Il Corriere della Sera* (still in print today). In the '30s, American comics, along with Italian productions, began being published in magazines such as *L'Avventuroso* (1934) and *L'Audace* (1935) and the medium opened its readership to young adults. Especially successful were the American adventure comics such as *Flash Gordon*, *Mandrake*, *The Phantom*, and the homegrown sci-fi of *Saturno contro la terra* (scripted by the future theorist of cinematic neorealism and *Bicycle Thief* screenwriter, Cesare Zavattini).

By 1938, in a country where illiteracy still possessed a large percentage of the population, *L'Avventuroso* sold nearly 600,000 copies per week, doubling the success of contemporary literary bestsellers such as those by Pitigrilli or Guido da Verona. Apart from a brief period of censorship (1938–1943) and a partial embargo aimed at American comics imposed by the Fascist regime, Italian publishers never adopted protectionist measures such as those imposed by France in the post-war years.

On the contrary, the strong presence of U.S. comics seemed to have stimulated local production. In fact, Italian authors absorbed their form and content and then reformulated them in an all-but-Mediterranean fashion (a similar trend emerged again in the '60s and '70s with the phenomenon of Italian genre cinema—especially with spaghetti westerns and crime movies).

An example of the cultural (and political) colonization Italy was undergoing at the time, Italian comics of the post-war years were mostly adventure comics, reflecting—and often—rewriting—many popular American genres, especially westerns (Tex, Pecos Bill, Kit Carson were among the most popular Italian comic book heroes of the time) and science fiction (particularly Superman, who, after a few short-lived name changes, was baptized Nembo Kid—possibly for copyright reasons or because the publishers in post-Fascist times were wary of involuntary Nietzschean references). Our authors' and intellectuals' love/hate relationship with everything American was, after all, one of the defining traits of our post-war cultural history. One has only to think of a paradigmatic figure such as Cesare Pavese, who first translated Melville's *Moby Dick*, or of the illustrious left-wing-leaning publishing house Einaudi that, from the immediate post-war years, introduced many American authors blacklisted by the Fascist regime to Italian audiences.

The first indications of a widening of readership age for comics appeared at the beginning of the '60s, thanks largely to the critical interest of theorists such as Umberto Eco and authors and intellectuals such as Italo Calvino and Elio Vittorini. Initially the subjects of serious critical analysis were mostly American strips. In *Apocalittici e integrati* (1964), Eco applied narratology and semiotics to Charles M. Schulz's *Peanuts* and Miton Caniff's *Steve Canyon*, and Calvino wrote his *Cosmicomiche* (1965) inspired by Johnny Hart's *B.C.*

But it is with the magazine *Linus* (1965), whose editorial board included authors and intellectuals such as Oreste del Buono and whose first issue hosted a round table on comic strips featuring Umberto Eco and Elio Vittorini, that Italian adult comics found an outlet and began to take shape. In the meantime, as comics became a delicacy for intellectuals and a playpen for budding semioticians, one of the most important events in the history of Italian adult comics had already developed: the phenomenon of the so-called "fumetti neri" (*black comics*).

• • •

Until the publication of the first issue of *Diabolik* (1962) by sisters Angela and Luciana Giussani, Italian comics were marketed exclusively to children and adolescents. The appearance and immediate success of a comic book whose hero, the mysterious Diabolik (fig. 1.1), was a cold-blooded criminal and in which homicide was constantly carried out with a considerable dose of sadism, revealed to many publishers the existence of an already available niche of adult readers for the medium. Thus, the genre *fumetto nero* was born.

Although the term *fumetti neri* was derived from the jargon of Italian journalism, where news is labeled as political, sport, pink (gossip), and black (crime), the early *Diabolik* stories were indebted to the tradition of *feuilletons*—in particular, to Pierre Souvestre and Marcel Allain's *Fantomas*, Maurice Leblanc's *Arsène Lupin*, and, in general, to the tradition of gothic. In fact, the explosion of *fumetti neri* was almost parallel to that which took place in Italian genre cinema: a tradition inaugurated by the gothic masterpieces of Riccardo Freda's *I vampiri* (1957), Giorgio Ferroni's *Il mulino delle donne di pietra* (1960), and Mario Bava's *La maschera del demonio* (1960), movies that opened the door for the long-lasting wave of horror and *giallo*[2] films running throughout the '70s and part of the '80s. Therefore, it made perfect sense that in 1968 it was Mario Bava himself who was called to direct a popular movie adaptation of *Diabolik*.

The instant success of *Diabolik* spawned an endless series of imitators, such as *Demoniak, Sadik, Zakimort, Masokis* (all sporting a *K* in *Diabolik* fashion!), *Fantasm, Tenebrax, Genius, Infernal*, and many others. But the most significant among this derivative horde of paper and ink villains were *Kriminal* and *Satanik*, both appearing in 1964 and both created by Roberto Raviola and Luciano Secchi under the pen names of Magnus and Bunker. *Kriminal* (fig. 1.2) and *Satanik* (fig. 1.3) introduced many innovations in the Italian comics landscape.

To begin with, they were the first publications to exhibit the "for adults" banner on their covers, therefore presenting themselves as comic books unquestionably intended for a mature audience. They were also the first to incorporate the touches of sadism that characterized *fumetti neri* with a conspicuous (for the time) dose of eroticism, thus opening the way for the more explicitly *sexy* comics that appeared en masse on Italian newsstands only a few years later.

In their best moments, both *Kriminal* and *Satanik* represent a true state of grace for Italian comics. The narrative ability of Secchi, a mediocre novelist but brilliant scriptwriter for comics (at least in the early days of his career), and the graphic strength of Raviola (who, a few years later, became one of the greatest signatures of European comics) united in a constant exchange of narrative intuitions. Moving with ease between picaresque, satirical, dramatic, and grotesque, Secchi and Raviola revealed a discursive depth quite unusual in Italian comics. Raviola's work in particular represented an important source of inspiration for key authors of the new Italian adult comics, such as Andrea Pazienza, Stefano Tamburini, and Filippo Scòzzari:

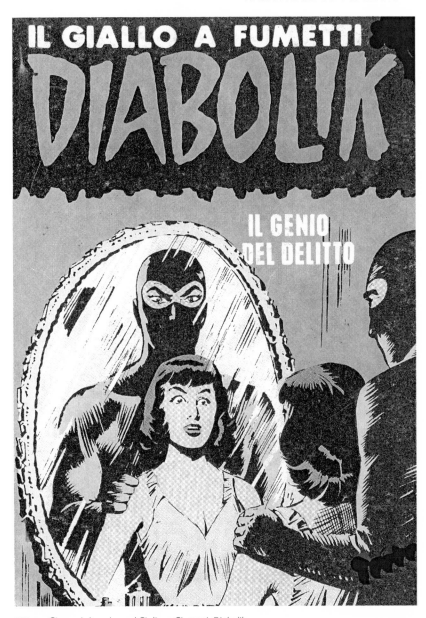

FIG. 1.1 Giussani, Angela, and Giuliana Giussani. *Diabolik*.

FIG. 1.2 Magnus (Roberto Raviola) and Bunker (Luciano Secchi). *Kriminal*. Magnus's drawing style of thick round lines and dense black shadows set the standard for all *fumetti neri*.

FIG. 1.3   Magnus and Bunker. *Satanik*. The female version of *Kriminal*, *Satanik* was the first example of a strong, amoral, sexually dominant heroine in Italian comics.

I cannot help but consider Magnus [Raviola] as a luminous figure. It is
not by chance that he was hated by the uptight and puritan editors of
Linus. The early *Kriminal* and *Satanik* stories were absolutely fantastic
because, from an artistic point of view, they represented an innovative
and rebellious slant in the context of the worn-out Italian comics scene.
They were ribald, and belligerent, both in their characters and in the way
they proposed themselves to the market. There's no doubt they were
satisfying a demand that had grown very strong. It was, really, the same
thing that happened ten years later, with much more effort, and without
the same editorial-industrial dimension, with our *Cannibale*. Magnus was
our forefather, a progenitor in front of which I humbly bow down in rev-
erence. (Scòzzari 2002, conversation with the author)

As a reaction to the enormous success of the *fumetti neri*, the year
1965 marked the beginning of a violent campaign against adult comics.
The result of this trial was a further divide in the medium—this time,
inside the trenches of the adult comics themselves. While publications
like *Diabolik*, *Kriminal*, and *Satanik* mitigated the violent and erotic component of their narratives, thus opening up to younger readers, others
marketed themselves even more directly to the adult readership. It was
the birth of the fumetti *vietati ai minori* (NC-16 rated comics).

From 1966 forward (for a period lasting approximately fifteen years)
more than a hundred publications appeared with content ranging from
the suggestively erotic to the blatantly pornographic. Among the most
popular, and the least amateurish, were *Jacula*, *Isabella* (a book that also
had a movie adaptation directed by Bruno Corbucci, brother of Sergio of
spaghetti western fame), *Vartàn*, *Lucifera*, *Lucrezia*, *Zora*, and *Hessa* (fig.
1.4, 1.5). For the most part, the *fumetti vietati* dabbled in the gothic and
horror genres, serving in equal parts gore and sexual situations (albeit
relatively tame ones, until the late '70s), making them the comic book
counterpart of the gothic and erotic movie phenomenon that developed
in Italy in the early '60s. Jacula and Zora were female vampires; Lucifera, a
demoness; Lucrezia, the infamous poison-bearing daughter of Pope Alessandro Borgia; and Hessa, an evil female SS officer.

To explain the appearance of the *fumetti neri* and *vietati ai minori* in
a country such as Italy where sexual matters were considered taboo and
which was, at the time, still strongly infused with Catholic morals, one
has to consider the radical changes the country was experiencing at the
end of the '50s—chiefly, the relaxing of censorship, which had been very

strict until the end of the decade. In this regard, the main contributing factors were the death of Pope Pio XII, whose austere pontificate (he had excommunicated the supporters of Communism worldwide in 1949) was followed by the more lenient one of his successor, Pope Giovanni XXIII; and the slight, but significant, decrease in the electoral results for the conservative Christian Democratic majority party that forced them into a more liberal center-left alliance.

Even more decisively, the *fumetti neri* and *vietati* phenomenon was a by-product of Italy's *miracolo economico*, the economic boom that—almost overnight, at the end of the '50s—changed Italian customs and society forever. As a result of the newfound economic wealth, new and old media prospered and developed. Television sets became affordable for most families, at least for those of the industrialized North; Cinecittà in Rome became the equivalent of a Mediterranean Hollywood; a modern music business was established, marketing mostly Italian versions of the latest American trends; and advertising became a pervasive and ubiquitous presence in the lives of the Italian people.

What's more—thanks to the opportunity for Italians to afford non-essential commodities, the increased literacy, and the consequent publishing boom—the newsstands were filled with a growing offering of newspapers, magazines, and, of course, comics. By the end of the '50s and during the following decade, the Italian mass media dramatically intensified the diversification of its target audience, a process of which the success of *fumetti neri* and *vietati* is highly paradigmatic.

Furthermore, the relaxing of censorship brought to the surface a large section of the collective imagination that had been deeply repressed. Paradoxically, the commoditization of sex as a by-product of the establishment of a modern consumerist society in Italy opened the doors for the sexual revolution of the late '60s and '70s, removing—by exorcising them—many of the taboos and repressive stigmas Catholicism and the bourgeois society had attached to the sexual sphere. As director Federico Fellini, himself a victim of censorship,[3] commented during a newspaper interview in 1968:

> Nowadays sex is less menacing, less troubling than how it was for our generation. Many taboos and moralistic deformation which transfigured desire have now fallen. This enormous diffusion of pornographic press reflects, after all, a revolt (certainly carnival-style) which follows a long period of moralistic repression, imposed by the Church through the

FIG. 1.4 Unknown artist. *Jacula.*

FIG. 1.5 Unknown artist. *Isabella*.

centuries. It is an intoxicating form of popularization of anything concerning the sexual sphere bordering on the abnormal, principally because this sphere was utterly forbidden. It is like the freedom of a prisoner or the appetite of somebody who fasted for a very long time. The excesses, the intemperance, are nothing but a reaction to the times in which sexual aspects of life were considered something to hide, to avoid, something you could not talk about. (*La Nazione*, May 10, 1968)

The fact that the majority of the protagonists of these titles were female shouldn't come as a surprise. Highly independent, sexually uninhibited, and substantially evil, the heroines of the *neri* and *vietati* represented, for the male readership, a way to exorcise the fear of women's emancipation the economic boom gradually put in motion. The Italian patriarchal society was slowly redefining its hierarchies—a transformation the Italian male was ill-equipped to deal with. It is not by coincidence that the same concerns were reflected in genre movies of the period. The star of the very first Italian horror, Franco Freda's *I Vampiri* (1956), is in fact a female vampire. In Mario Bava's gothics, murderers and monsters are often female, as exemplified by his *La maschera del demonio* in which Barbara Steele plays the double role of the positive character: a chaste castle dweller (a prototypical housewife)—and the negative one: a vengeful and lusty witch.[4] Likewise, a decade later in the movies of the godfather of the *giallo*, Dario Argento, the assassin is almost invariably revealed to be a woman.

Frequently dismissed in the histories of Italian comics, the *neri* and *vietati* publications, although often marred by below-average artwork and simple-minded plots, have a specific relevance because with their appearance Italian comics irreversibly cut ties with an image of childhood-only entertainment.[5] In the eye of public opinion, not only had comics become potentially evil and harmful, but some also became alternative publications: semi-clandestine, something to buy—and hide. Some newsstand owners refused to carry them, some kept them hidden, and one can only imagine the stashed-away collections discovered and disposed of by scandalized parents (I hid mine behind a pile of *Donald Duck* comics and they were never found!). Once the great taboo of sex had been broken, comics became potentially free to open themselves to virtually any subject.

While the *neri* and *vietati* did their "dirty" work with truck drivers, drafted soldiers, and teenagers alike, in the world of "official" culture, intellectuals like Vittorini, Calvino and Eco—some on the pages of *Quaderni*

FIG. 1.6 The cover of the first issue of *Linus*.

di Semiotica, some from those of *Linus*—suggested comics could require reading strategies as complex and satisfying as those one could adopt for a Faulkner or Conrad novel. It was the birth of the school of *auteur* comics that consolidated itself in the early '70s.

A revolution akin to the American underground comics of the late '60s (epitomized by such titles as Robert Crumb's *Zap*, Gilbert Shelton's *The Fabulous Furry Freak Brothers*, and Greg Irons's *Deviant Slice*) did not occur in Italy until a decade later with the new adult comics. Such destabilizing function had instead been exerted by the *neri* and *vietati*, although in a minor key and in a much more popular context. The adult comics proper, and, subsequently, the school of auteur comics, developed with the appearance of magazines such as *Linus* (1965) and its derivatives, e.g., *Eureka* (1968, edited by *Kriminal* and *Satanik* creator Secchi) and *Il Mago* (1972). *Linus* (fig. 1.6), in particular, aimed for the educated reader sympathetic to the official Italian left wing.

From its beginnings, along with a selection of more or less politically engaged American strips (Walt Kelly's *Pogo*, Garry Trudeau's *Doonesbury*, along with Schulz's *Peanuts* and Hart's *B.C.*), *Linus* published Italian authors such as Hugo Pratt, Dino Battaglia, and Guido Crepax. And though this new wave of Italian comic artists is generally referred to as a *school*, their poetics and background were actually quite diverse.

The most popular of this group was Hugo Pratt, who also had a strong European following, especially in France. Pratt concentrated exclusively on adventure stories and while his references in the world of comics are drawn mostly from Milton Caniff's seminal '40s strip *Terry and the Pirates* (at least in the early part of his career), he also borrowed from classic nineteenth-century adventure novels, especially from Robert Louis Stevenson, Joseph Conrad, Herman Melville, and James Fenimore Cooper. Though adventure comics had always been popular childhood entertainment in Italy, Pratt read his sources with a depth quite novel to the comic book medium up to that point, i.e., stressing themes such as rites of passage from childhood to adulthood (both Stevenson's *Kidnapped*[6] and Conrad's *The Shadow Line* must have been favorite readings), the effects of colonialism, and the clash between human laws and natural order.

Pratt's groundbreaking work was *La ballata del mare salato* (The Ballad of the Salty Sea), which began in 1967 in his own magazine, *Sgt. Kirk*. *La ballata del mare salato* introduced his most popular character, the sailor Corto Maltese (fig 1.7), and is notable not only for the art, storytelling,

FIG. 1.7 Pratt, Hugo. *La ballata del mare salato.*

and its attention to geographical and historical accuracy (although Pratt managed to feature Rasputin the Monk as Corto Maltese's antagonist in a story set in the south seas), but also for being, at almost 200 pages, the longest adult comic book story published in Italy up to that point. A precursor to the modern *graphic novel*, Pratt's epic set the standard for all adult adventure comics of the decade; it is not surprising that his work was the first of the adult comics to be republished in the early '70s in luxurious hardcover editions aimed at bookstores rather than newsstands.

Like Pratt, Dino Battaglia was a skilled illustrator and storyteller with roots in nineteenth-century literature as demonstrated by his adaptations of short stories by Guy de Maupassant, Edgar Allan Poe, and E.T.A. Hoffmann, as well as his gothic rendition of Melville's *Moby Dick*. Also of note is Battaglia's adaptation of Rabelais's *Gargantua and Pantagruel*, one of his most ambitious projects that, curiously enough, he published in the pages of the Catholic comic book magazine *Il Giornalino* in 1975. Although, graphically, his references lie mostly in nineteenth-century illustration rather than comics, Battaglia remains one of the most-loved adult comics authors of the decade.

Guido Crepax might be considered the most revolutionary of the group. Different in style and themes from either Pratt or Battaglia, Crepax was much indebted to the French adult comics developing at that time (especially Claude Forest's *Barbarella*), the cinematic *nouvelle vague* of Godard and Truffaut, and American pop art. Crepax's pop-imbued aesthetics derived from his stint in the graphic advertising business before he began his career in comics (in 1957 his campaign for Shell Oil won him a Gold Palm for advertisement).

With *Valentina*, his most popular character, Crepax introduced erotica to highbrow adult comics. Conceived in 1965 and serialized in *Linus*, *Valentina* developed through the years from a pop-character battling against and alongside superheroes, secret agents, witches, etc., to an elegant erotic saga with Freudian undertones, shifting between realism and oneiric suggestions as the character slowly morphed into an ordinary middle-aged, middle-class woman.

Crepax's most important innovation was his reformulation of the comic page grid as a result of his interest in reproducing the kinetic effect of cinematic montage within the static medium of comics (fig. 1.8). In particular, the intricate constructions of Crepax's pages replicate the choppy editing and irregular framing of early *nouvelle vague* films. The busy fragmentation of the action and multiplication of point of view in a series of panels of uneven sizes mimics cinema's own variable length of shots. An anti-Hollywoodian practice of storytelling, Crepax's work featured arhythmical sequences that read like graphic counterparts of the post-tonal music of the twentieth century and is diametrically opposite to classic adventure comics such as Herge's *Tintin* or Jacob's *Blake and Mortimer*.

In addition to Pratt, Battaglia, and Crepax, other important authors represented an in-between generation. Of these, the most notable is Guido Buzzelli (fig. 1.9), not only for the quality of his art and storytelling, but also because his work anticipated by a wide margin the new adult comics of the late '70s and '80s. Buzzelli was the first of the '70s auteurs to immigrate to comics from the world of high-art having started his career as a painter, a path that would become less uncommon among the Italian comic book artists of the '80s.

Much more adult in look and themes than that of his colleagues, Buzzelli's work is marked by a pervasive grotesque mood, the effectiveness of which is underscored by his realistic drawing style. His stories engaged challenging topics: class struggle, science, and ethics (in his allegorical I

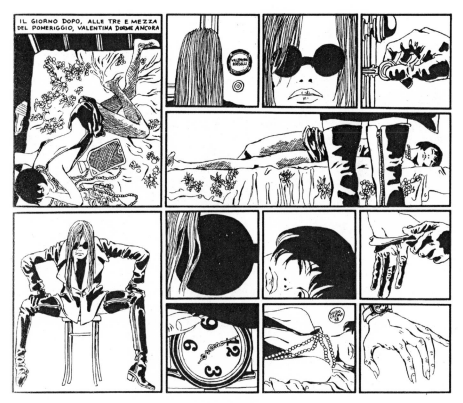

FIG. 1.8 Crepax, Guido. *Valentina.*

labirinti [*Labyrinths*] the world is taken over by surgeons led by a Christiaan Barnard-like figure), and the widening gap between body and self in contemporary society (in *Zil Zelub*, an anagram of the author's name, the protagonist loses control of his limbs, which abandon him to satisfy pent-up urges).

Taking distance from both Pratt's adventure genre and Crepax's pop eroticism, Buzzelli's comics are situated halfway between pataphysical theatre and apologue on modern society. Perhaps too innovative for the Italian audience, Buzzelli's works were at first published in France and only a few years later appeared in the pages of *Linus*'s supplement, *Alter Linus*.

Just as grotesque (although with a lighter approach) and as adult with his references and materials is the work of Marco Tullio Altan, who began his career in *Linus* in the mid-'70s. Altan's most important works are the

FIG. 1.9 Buzzelli, Guido. *I labirinti.*

debunking and caricatural, but historically accurate, biographies of Christopher Columbus, Giacomo Casanova, and Saint Francis of Assisi. Among his characters, his most popular is the communist factory worker Cipputi, protagonist of many of his political one-panel cartoons for various magazines and newspapers. Altan also worked extensively outside the circuit of adult comics and so far has published more than fifty children's books.

Among the generation of authors that sprang up in the early '70s, the most commercially successful and most translated abroad was Milo Manara. Manara began his career illustrating *fumetti vietati* (*Jolanda de Almaviva*) and graduated to auteur status in the mid-'70s with an allegorical fictional biography of chairman Mao Tze Tung (*Lo Scimmiotto*), also in *Alter Linus*. His works soon evolved into elegant, if somewhat repetitive, erotic narratives with various exotic settings (South America, Africa, India, etc.) and incorporated "high" literary references to authors such as Jorge Luis Borges and Luigi Pirandello.

Of note are his two collaborations with Federico Fellini (a comic book enthusiast and a cartoonist himself), both in the director's final years. The first, *Viaggio a Tulum*, appeared in 1986; the second and final one was supposed to be the completed version of *Il viaggio di G. Mastorna*, the movie Fellini had attempted to make during most of his career (the autobiographical *Eight and a Half* refers to the director's failure to start the production of this very film).

Curiously, due to Fellini's illness and a bizarre printing accident when the comic was serialized in the magazine *il Grifo*, even the comic book version was left unfinished. The next two installments would have told of Mastorna's travels in the afterlife, but due to a printing mistake, the word *END* appeared at the bottom of the last page of the first episode. The always-superstitious Fellini then decided it was a good place to stop and withdrew from the project. *Il viaggio di G. Mastorna* is to this day considered by many Italian film critics the most famous never-filmed movie in the history of cinema.

To understand in full the development of adult comics in the mid-'60s and its relative countermovement at the end of the '70s and into the following decade, it is necessary to observe the Italian cultural and political situation of the time. By 1965, when *Linus* debuted, Italian society was experiencing the full effects of the economic boom and coming to terms with the sudden traumatizing changes it introduced. As mentioned earlier, the results of increased economic prosperity were the disappearance of rural culture, mass migration to the big cities, the emergence of a new middle class (especially in the industrial north), the establishment of a modern consumerist society, rising literacy, the relaxing of censorship, and the developing impact of mass media, such as print, television, and cinema.

However, two decades after the end of WWII, the country was still politically tied to a post-war and Cold-War climate. One should not forget that the Italian Republic was, after all, virtually born out of what was essentially a civil war that took place during the last phase of WWII and that saw the struggle of the resistance fighters against the remains of the Fascist regime.

Indeed, the elections of 1948, which were closely monitored by the U.S. (concerned Italy would fall under the influence of the eastern block[7])— represented the missed turning point the left wing had envisioned for Italian society and the crystallization of a political status quo that dragged on nearly four decades. With the narrow victory of the center-right Christian Democratic party (greatly advantaged not only by American pressures and propaganda and by the vocal support of the Vatican,[8] but also by the untimely Communist *coup* in Prague in February) and the defeat of the Communist Party, the country found itself split in two.

The Christian Democratic party governed Italy uninterrupted (though often through a series of alliances with minority parties) until 1982 and the Communist Party became the main opposition. Throughout those decades, a tacit pact allowed that while the Christian Democrats retained political power, the Communists had almost complete control on cultural areas (with the exception of infrastructures, such as TV and radio, whose monopoly belonged exclusively to the State until 1975). As a result, the great majority of intellectuals, including directors, writers, and painters gravitated towards the left wing where, almost exclusively, cultural debate thrived well into the '80s. Consider the importance of cultural phenomena such as literary neorealism, first centered on the partisans' fight against the Fascist and Nazi occupation forces and later on the working-class struggles in northern industrialized cities—and central figures such as Elio Vittorini, Italo Calvino, Cesare Pavese, Alberto Moravia, Luchino Visconti, and Pier Paolo Pasolini (all intellectuals at one point tied to the Communist Party). Although the Soviet Union's invasion of Hungary in 1956 and the Italian Communist Party's refusal to condemn the intervention caused many intellectuals to distance themselves from the Party, many remained involved in left-wing politics. It is no surprise then that when comics became *adult*—joining the outer fringes of official culture—they surfaced (one might say, they were co-opted) in the milieu of left-wing culture and in publications aimed at a left-wing readership such as *Linus*.

A concern central to the relationship between cultural engagement and the Communist Party of the time was the role of intellectuals, and art in general, as a pedagogical instrument aimed at building politically and class-conscious citizens. This notion, greatly simplified, derived from the formulations of Marxist intellectual Antonio Gramsci in his *Quaderni del Carcere*, and was taken to extremes by the Party, which eventually espoused Zhdanovist[9] positions.

Many left-wing intellectuals early in the post-war years disagreed with the Party and warned against the dangers of reducing art to a mere political and didactical instrument. Vittorini, for example, was one of the first to voice these concerns and distance himself from the official Left: "The role of the intellectual is not that of banging the drum for the revolution," was his reply in the pages of his journal, *Il politecnico*, to Communist Party secretary Palmiro Togliatti as early as 1947.

That notwithstanding, a palpable degree of Zhdanovism, of didacticism, and a focus on content—social and political—rather than on intrinsic structural values, continued in the following decades. In a way, only popular art, since it was a mere product, remained completely immune to this co-opting of ideological commitment. Given this premise, one may even say, albeit with a polemical intent, that Italian genre movies and *fumetti neri* and *vietati*, although tied to the laws of demand their markets imposed and with their obvious limitations, were paradoxically the most independent and spontaneous among our cultural output between the '50s and '70s.

In this climate, the question of the culturally and politically ambiguous position of adult comics, by now a legitimate periphery of official culture, became extremely problematic. On this subject, the case of *Linus* is certainly paradigmatic. Almost from its inception, its readership was primarily left-wing supporters, either independent or tied to the Communist Party—comic book aficionados who enjoyed the Italian and American Golden-Age reprints, those mostly interested in progressive American political strips such as *Doonesbury* and Feiffer's one-pagers, and those who enjoyed the new Italian *maestros* such as Pratt, Crepax, and Battaglia. However, most of them superimposed a strict ideological reading on *Linus*'s offerings (one which the editorial staff encouraged to a certain extent). Walt Kelly's *Pogo*, for example, was regarded as a strip with strong leftist innuendos, as were, by way of bizarre hermeneutical strategies, Al Capp's *Li'l Abner* and Hart's *B.C.*

Among the Italian auteurs, Crepax's *Valentina* was loved for its Freudian undertones, but also because its eponymous heroine was a liberated middle-class woman defying bourgeois conventions (not to mention her passion for Leon Trotsky). Battaglia was accepted and respected for the high literary tone he gave to his works, as was Pratt's *Corto Maltese*—not only because it rewrote the adventure canon from the perspective of losers and minorities—but because the genre benefited from a sort of ideological immunity.

For this reason, the editors decided to inaugurate a supplement, *Alter Linus*, which would host everything that couldn't fit in the more politicized *Linus*: adventure comics, new European authors, and early French adult comics (*Barbarella*, whose explicit eroticism had not met the favors of early readers of the magazine[10], and the equally risqué *Paulette* by Lob and Pichard). But in the mid-'70s, when the magazine dared publish a run of Chester Gould's *Dick Tracy* (one of the most important American strips of the '40s and '50s), the readers demanded and obtained the strip's removal, accusing Gould's work of blatantly espousing Fascist ideologies (would *Li'l Abner* have remained so popular had the readers been aware of its author's right-wing leanings?). In short, few escaped ideological scrutiny.

This attitude of being "either with us or against us" was the direct result of the Cold-War atmosphere of the time. The conservative, Christian

Democratic-led government—standing for American capitalism, repressive Catholic morals, patriarchal family values, censorship, etc.—was pitted against the progressive Marxist left. Although fragmentation among left-wing supporters occurred (first as a result of the Hungarian invasion of '56, then with the protests of '68), intellectuals and artists had nowhere else to go. As a result, the school of auteur comic artists found it hard to renew its poetics and gradually closed in on itself.

Many like Pratt safely practiced the adventure genre; others like Crepax slid into an empty repetition of forms and soliloquy. Even the movement of '68, the student protests, and the development of a new unofficial left did not contribute to alter this state of affairs; if anything, the Cold-War polarization intensified. Only a decade later, concomitantly with the second wave of student protests of '77, there was a sudden and decisive shift—one swiftly portrayed by the new adult comics.

Unbeknownst to readers, Italian and French adult comics lived parallel lives for most of the '60s; however, publishers, editors, and artists were aware of each other, and the importance of the resulting reciprocal influence cannot be stressed enough. Appearing in the pages of the French periodical *V-magazine* as early as 1962, Forest's *Barbarella* (fig. 1.10) can be considered the first adult European comic of the '60s *tout court*—and maybe the first adult comic, *period*. Fittingly, *Barbarella* also appeared in the debut issue of *Linus*, and it's not hard to see the influence the character had on the development of *Linus*'s own heroine, Valentina. Similarly, while the influential French magazine *Charlie* (1969) began as something of a tribute to its Italian counterpart *Linus*, by the '70s the works of *Charlie*'s French comic artists, such as Copi, Wolinski, and Bretécher, began appearing in *Linus*. Moreover, the great majority of the Italian auteurs, including Pratt, Battaglia, Buzzelli, and Manara, found a welcoming audience and willing publishers in France where their works were printed both in periodicals and in luxurious hardcover editions.[11]

In France, the first hints of adult comics are found within anthology magazines such as *Pilote* (1959). Although *Pilote* published mostly adventure stories geared toward younger readers, its contributors often slipped in references aimed at a more mature audience, such as the allegory of Nazi occupation in Rene Goscinny's *Asterix* and the individualist and antimilitarist message in Jean Giraud's *Blueberry*. During these years, French comics, unlike their Italian counterparts, developed along their own lines with almost no American influences. The reason is partly to be found in a protectionist law promulgated in 1949 that limited the publication of

FIG. 1.10 Forest, Jean-Claude. *Barbarella*. A painterly style and a strong surrealist sensibility contributed to the innovative drive of *Barbarella*, Forest's best-known comic book saga.

foreign comics. Although this rule, voted by the communist government of the time, was masked by moralizing intentions aimed at the safety of young readers, the intention and result was to prevent the diffusion of American comics and what was perceived to be their treacherous capitalist-imperialist ideology.

Barbarella's futuristic scantily clad space adventurer was inspired by the figure of Brigitte Bardot, and her stories were explicitly geared toward an adult audience. Not only did *Barbarella* often include sexual situations (some of them decidedly risqué for the times), but, even more notably, Forest's work introduced the inversion of hierarchies between plot and visual rendition, between story and discourse—to use Seymour Chatman's formulation,[12] which became the trademark of French and Italian adult comics in the following decade. It was a trend Crepax pioneered in Italy with his *Valentina* and that evolved in the rhetoric inherent in many of the works of the *postmodern* adult comics of the late '70s and '80s.

Forest's graphic style, with its suggestions deriving from the world of painting, especially French surrealism, has a notable estranging function in relation to the plot: it rewrites it, freezes it by demanding to be observed and studied, and subtly makes it the target of an ironic discourse (the importance of which will be discussed in the following chapters). While, for example, in Will Eisner's *The Spirit*, the complex and conspicuous visual devices are nonetheless always rigorous functions of the plot, in

Forest's work the relationship is inverted—it is the visionary surge that demands of the plot the means to come to fruition. Consequently, *Barbarella*'s genre, science-fiction, became a pretext for a graphic flux which embraced not only surrealist painting, but also book illustration of the nineteenth century, art deco, and pop art techniques. A few years later in 1964, Forest launched his own adult comics magazine, *Chouchou*, hosting artists such as Paul Gillon, Pichard (*Paulette*), and Forest himself.

Although *Barbarella* can be considered the first adult comic, the first adult comic *magazine*—*Hara Kiri*—had appeared two years earlier in 1960. *Hara Kiri* was chiefly a satirical publication and hosted mostly vignettes and one-pagers. On first sight, it might have appeared to be an adult-oriented derivate of the American *Mad*, but on closer scrutiny its humor was much more virulent, verging on calculated bad taste (and in fact its subtitle read: "the stupid and evil magazine"). Among the staff of *Hara Kiri* were Georges Wolinski; the French surrealist Roland Topor (also a novelist, scriptwriter, animator, and actor); the genial Jean-Marc Reiser; and Jean Giraud, under the pseudonym Moebius.

Hara Kiri, namely because of its cynicism and outrageous poetics, later became a model for the Italian authors of *Cannibale* (1977) and *Il Male* (1978), and some of its materials were eventually republished by the Italian magazine *L'Arcibraccio*. In 1970, *Hara Kiri* was permanently banned by the French authorities for making fun of General Charles de Gaulle's death, and its staff migrated en masse to the pages of *Charlie*. *Hara Kiri* spawned other publications, also satirical and just as vitriolic, notably, two institutions of French adult comics: *L'Echo des Savanes* (1972) and *Fluide Glacial* (1975).

Among the French adult comics periodicals of the '70s, the most innovative, the most idiosyncratic, and the one that had the most influence on Italian artists was, without a doubt, *Metal Hurlant* (1975). The comics in *Metal Hurlant* differed radically from those of the Italian adult *auteurs* of the '60s and '70s—for starters, they introduced a marked sense of humor that the Italians, often lost in the seriousness of their references (be it Freudian and Marxist theory or the American and European nineteenth-century literary classics), distinctly lacked. Most importantly, the *Humanoids* (as the authors comprising the staff of *Metal Hurlant* called themselves) aimed to destabilize the narrative rigidity that marked both the Italian and the classic Belgian school (the latter based on the logic of constant narrative rhythms and cause-and-effect relationships that constituted the discursive backbone of influential classics such as *Tintin* and

Blake and Mortimer). More than any other, the work that stands as a declaration of the focus of the group is Moebius's *Hermetic Garage*, featuring
a narration that reproduces the effect of TV surfing (or Internet surfing,
for that matter) and a hyper-production of narrative levels, highly diverse
graphic styles,[13] sudden stylistic turns, and ironic innuendos.

> There's no need for a story to be like a house with a door as an entrance,
> windows to watch trees from, and a chimney for the smoke. . . . One can
> instead imagine a story in the shape of an elephant, or a cornfield, or the
> flame of a match. (Moebius interviewed by Jean-Pierre Dionnet, *Alter
> Linus*, June, 1978, 97)

It is evident that Moebius's declaration of independence on behalf of
the author not only recalls the European historical avant-gardes, but also
the narrative formulations of contemporary authors of the OuLiPo group,
such as Raymond Queneau, and the experience of the *nouveau roman*.
Metal Hurlant left its mark in French comics thanks also to outstanding
artists and unconventional storytellers, such as Yves Chaland, Caro, and
Loustal, and it had significant impact in Italy when *Alter Linus* began publishing its works in 1977.

In the pages of *Metal Hurlant* the first significant dialogue between
media—pop music, fashion, cinema, literature—occurred, which tightly
connected comics to an active web of cultural systems. In other words,
comics, aside from political and satirical ones, started replicating and
reformulating the present—an option impracticable for the Italian
auteurs. The possibility of a mimetic opening to present times suggested
by the Humanoids was immediately picked up by the Italian authors of
Cannibale and *Frigidaire*, the main magazines of the new Italian adult
comics.

Comics continue to be treated with great respect in France (one has
only to enter a French bookstore where comics are neatly ordered by publisher, side by side with literary works), but a severe crisis in the industry
at the end of the '80s saw the disappearance of a number of venerable
publications such as *Metal Hurlant*, *A Suivre*, and *L'Echo des Savanes*. This
crisis coincided chronologically with one in Italy.

By the mid-'70s, magazines like *Linus* and the increasing success of
the homegrown school of auteurs had created a three-way split in comics, almost involuntarily replicating that strict division of levels (popular
vs. elitist, art vs. entertainment) that existed for other media. On one

side, there were comics for the very young (*Topolino, Tiramolla, Soldino*—the ones published in the still-popular *Corriere dei Piccoli*, etc.) and the adventure stories aimed at a young audience, but also widely read by older readers (mostly westerns such as *Tex, Zagor, Il piccolo ranger*, etc.). On the adult side there were the under-the-radar and virtually free (but rarely qualitatively satisfying) *fumetti vietati*, and finally the highbrow *auteur* comics, with their innovations and subtleties, but also with their implicit censorships (self-imposed or not) and their increasing difficulty relating to a changing society and a political situation that was approaching the stormy upheavals of '77. However, between the slapdash attitude of the *vietati* and the elitism of the *auteurs* there were some grey areas, and it is here the roots of the adult comics authors of the following generation are to be found.

The most important link between the comics of the '60s and those of the post-'77 era is the work by Magnus and Bunker. When the season of *fumetti neri* ended around the late '60s, the pair interrupted their work on *Satanik* and *Kriminal* and issued their most influential creation: *Alan Ford* (1968), a humorous secret agent farce spoofing a genre made popular in those years by the 007 movies. *Alan Ford* (fig. 1.11) gracefully managed to be a transversal publication: its brand of humor made it suitable for a young audience; the quality of the art, the grotesque undertones, and the adult asides made it appealing to the discriminating grown-up readership; and its format—small pocket-size and a two-panel page grid, along with Magnus's already-familiar art, his signature heavy blacks, and sensual round, thick lines promising mischief and forbidden thrills, made it a success also with the *vietati* readers.

However, *Alan Ford*'s truly innovative characteristic was the style Magnus devised for it. Halfway between the artsy realism of the auteur comics and the cartoonish style of children's comics, *Alan Ford*'s art mixed the debased world of satire and picaresque with that of sentiment and tragedy so that its grotesque tones were constantly questioned by its realism, and vice versa. This graphic-narrative style was something quite novel not only for Italian comics, but also rather unusual in our twentieth-century artistic output, with Carlo Emilio Gadda and Tommaso Landolfi in the literary canon, and some cinematic works of Elio Petri, Carlo Lizzani, and Pier Paolo Pasolini being among the few exceptions. An illustrious predecessor displaying an equally complex modal narrative approach was Will Eisner's *The Spirit* and, in fact, Secchi's magazine *Eureka* was the first to introduce his stories in Italy.

FIG. 1.11   Magnus and Bunker. *Alan Ford*. An understated masterpiece of Swiftian black humor and the grotesque, *Alan Ford* was one of the best-selling Italian comics of the early '70s. The balloons read: "Alms for the poor, kind sir. Alms for the poor children dying of hunger." "What are you blubbering about, kid? Of course they're dying of hunger, they're poor!"

The political upheaval of '68 didn't substantially alter the climate of strict ideological pressure diffused both in the adult comic world and in other cultural areas. There were, however, besides the successful *Alan Ford*, some notable exceptions, mostly publications tied to the counterculture and the new independent left that emerged as a result of the widening gap between the Communist Party and the younger generations. Generally satirical and political in context, the comics appearing in these publications introduced a verve and sense of freedom the official adult comics lacked.

Among the many, it is worth mentioning *Re Nudo*, a magazine of the young extra-parliamentary new left which, along with articles on politics, music, eastern religions, sexual education, and debates on drugs (both topics considered taboo in the Italian press of the time), published what could be considered the Italian version of American underground comics. Among the many authors that contributed to the magazine was a young Scòzzari, one of the main authors of the new adult comics of the late '70s and '80s and future editor of *Cannibale* and *Frigidaire*. Also appearing in the early '70s was the short-lived, but highly influential *L'Arcibraccio*, which introduced in Italy the vitriolic artwork of the French authors of *Hara Kiri*.

Finally, an important outlet for unorthodox comics was *L'Avventurista*,[14] the supplement to the newspaper of the independent left, *Lotta Continua*. *Lotta Continua* was one of the many far-left extra-parliamentary groups born as a result of the Italian '68. Although the group decided to terminate its activity in 1976, having acknowledged the failure of collective action that brought forth the new configurations of autonomous collectives of '77, the newspaper continued publication until 1982. Between '77 and '78 *Lotta Continua* published a satirical insert edited by the cartoonist Vincino. When the venture folded under the strain of repeated censorship from the newspaper's editorial board, Vincino moved its artists into a new publication, *Il Male*—one of the most important satirical magazines of the new adult comics.

All these publications foreshadowed the rise of the independent press, a completely new phenomenon for Italy that characterized many aspects of the protest movement of '77 (Stampa Alternativa being among one of the most active independent publishers at that time). The new adult comics were born in this environment and took their first steps in the pages of the independently published *Re Nudo, Combinzioni, Il Male*, and *Cannibale*. A long way from the *auteur* comics because of their background, look, and readership, these comics signaled a drastic change for the medium and mirrored the deep changes brought about by the Italian '77.

CHAPTER TWO

The Emergence of the Second Generation of Adult Comics in Its Political Context

The radical rewriting of codes the new adult comics were to enact on their medium—the intense dialogue between the high and low end of the cultural spectrum, their tendency towards intertextuality as well as cultural horizontality—are all tightly linked to the climate of social and political unrest that characterized the second half of the '70s in Italy. Born in the midst of the '77 student protest movement, the second generation of adult comics was deeply influenced by, and, in turn, influenced the concomitant explosion of new counterculture media: the independent press, free radio, and alternative music. The exchange of ideas and languages between these areas was so close that any attempt to analyze the extent of the innovations brought forth by the adult comics without placing them in this wider context would be flawed.

By the late '70s, not only were the coordinates of both the antagonist culture and its official counterpart rapidly changing, but the disillusionment with the outcomes of '68 and the development of new social and economic assets were giving shape to a different audience of adult comics and counterculture in general, a new entity the puzzled sociologists of the times called the *new social subject*. Since this emerging social stratum, along with the spontaneous political movement it generated, provided the audience and the breeding ground from which the authors of the new adult comics would spring, it is necessary to carefully scrutinize the factors that brought about its existence.

In the summer of 1976, the counterculture magazine *Re Nudo*, in coordination with extra-parliamentary groups such as *Lotta Continua*, the first autonomous groups (most of which fell under the label "Autonomia"), and various anarchist collectives, organized its second summer festival at Parco Lambro, a park area on the outskirts of Milan. The patent failure of what was meant to be the most important gathering of the new proletarian youth was the first warning sign that things had drastically changed from the days of collective action of '68. This is how comic artist Filippo Scòzzari, at the time in the ranks of *Re Nudo* and among the founders of the magazine *Cannibale*, remembers the Festival of Parco Lambro in his autobiography *Prima pagare, poi ricordare*:

> The willingness that the staff of *Re Nudo* had for publishing my artwork more or less echoed their ability for understanding reality, and unfortunately for them, reality slapped them in the face. June 26, 27, 28, 29. The attendance was way beyond their expectations (one hundred thousand people), but that was not their fault. Their fault was failing to realize that their *young proletarians* were bored, angry, frustrated, and poor and that locking all of them in the enclosed limits of the Lambro park was like pushing thirty lab rats in a shoe box, shaking it, and standing there to watch. Fights between groups, proletarian expropriations in nearby supermarkets. Police. Tear gas. Heroin. Thefts between comrades. (Scòzzari, *Prima pagare, poi ricordare*, 24)

Another example of the way in which the events were reported by a 1976 article that appeared in the independent journal *A/traverso*:

> Some were raiding the stands of their own comrades, some destroyed the stand of the gay rights association Cony, some groups were molesting women shouting "men of Parco Lambro charge!" The violence of impotence came face to face with the impotence of violence and all the tensions were released in this ghetto where proletarian expropriation was substituted by its own spectacle. (*A/traverso*, July, 1976)

The failure of the Parco Lambro festival attracted great attention from both the official press and the independent small-circulation publications of the movement. Of course, the right-wing press didn't miss out either and they capitalized on the events by demonizing the new left. But few caught the real meaning of the event: that the disastrous outcome of the festival was the symptom of a radical change in the composition of what was still referred to, somewhat anachronistically, as *proletarian youth*.[1]

At the heart of the matter was the failure of the extra-parliamentary groups and the collective action that characterized much of the protests of the '68 movement, as well as the appearance of a new generation of students and workers who saw as alien both the strict ideological models these earlier groups adopted and their implicit third-internationalist stances. As early as 1973, with the strike at the Mirafiori factory,[2] the groups had begun to show their limits and contradictions. In the same year, the events at Mirafiori led to the disbandment of Toni Negri's *Potere Operaio*.[3]

This situation continued to ripen until 1976 with the end of one of the other main extra-parliamentary groups that sprang out of the turmoil of '68, Adriano Sofri's *Lotta Continua* (although their journal of the same name continued publishing for a few years).[4] By the end of 1976, the horizon of the extra-parliamentary groups was replaced by a substantially spontaneous and anti-hierarchical movement characterized by a markedly diverse social composition. If the movement of '68 in Italy had been the result of a never-before-seen, albeit brief, synergy between middle-class students and the working class, what became the Movement (with a capital M hereafter) of '77 introduced a greater ambiguity concerning class identification.

The recent economic transformations in Italy and the increased fluidity in the job market had created an environment in which work activity was not only precarious and temporary, but also interchangeable between manual and intellectual (Balestrini 531), therefore making obsolete the divide between middle and working class, at least for urban youth. In this regard, the great diversity of the participants at the Parco Lambro Festival should have been a herald to the analysts of the time. The factory, too, from the mid-'70s, began losing its centrality, both economically and as a source of political action, and Italy began its journey toward that model first defined as post-capitalism by Daniel Bell as early as 1973 in his *The Coming of Post-Industrial Society*, and then by Frederic Jameson in his *Postmodernism, or, the Cultural Logic of Late Capitalism* (1992).

As a result of the great economic crisis affecting both manual and intellectual work, new and class-ambiguous social niches started to appear. Rising in unemployment, the growing number of college students, in combination with the increasing scarcity of jobs for university graduates, created an increasingly diverse urban proletariat that turned down factory work and *lavoro garantito* (protected employment covered by pension schemes and social security), preferring instead short-term work or the occasional odd job.

A parallel phenomenon tied to the birth of the Movement was the appearance, approximately in 1975, of *centri sociali*, "squats." The taking over of abandoned suburban buildings to use as social spaces for festivals, laboratories, cultural activities, and political debates spread so fast that at the end of 1976 Italy counted more than a hundred of them, with the majority in the north. Squats played a decisive role in configuring the schizophrenic identity that characterized the Movement, as they were the point of confluence for unemployed youths from the suburbs, ex-members of groups such as Potere Operaio and Lotta Continua, middle-class students, and anarchists. They also had great importance as a place for diffusion of the counterculture through the Movement's press, alternative music, and comics.

The Parco Lambro festival somehow laid bare all the diversity, contradictions, and frustrations that had accumulated in this section of society at the dawn of the Italian '77: the great abyss that had opened between youth proletariat and the Communist Party; the refusal, especially after the electoral defeats of 1975, of the ideologies and power structures underlying the agenda of the extra-parliamentary groups and new *partitini* "small parties"; and the birth of a political consciousness focused on the private sphere and individual action:

> "The new collective groups of '77 were very distant from the third-internationalist idea of a master-party, they were not formed to erase, but to encourage freedom, creativity, ingenuity, irony, and the independent thinking of authors, narrators, writers, and journalists." (Sparagna in Mordente, *Stefano Tamburini* 9)

The epicenter of both the '77 student protests and the development of the new adult comics was the wealthy middle-class city of Bologna—the comic artists Pazienza, Scòzzari, Corona, Carpinteri, Jori, Igort (Igor Tuveri), and the precursors, Magnus and Bonvi, all lived there. At the same time, Bologna was also the home of the collective *A/traverso*; one of the first free radios, Radio Alice; and a growing independent music scene. The reason for this confluence of activities is to be found in Bologna's status as the most illustrious college city in Italy, home of the oldest European university (hence the nickname *Bologna la dotta*, Bologna the learned). Furthermore, in the '70s, with the opening of Umberto Eco's DAMS, a college division dedicated to semiotics and the study of mass media, Bologna became the magnet for an array of creative-minded students, a great number of which were *fuorisede* "non-resident" and a relevant percentage coming from abroad.

This mingling of cultures bore its fruit by the end of the '70s, and it is no surprise that Bologna became the home of what has been described as "the creative side of the Movement." In reality, the first instance of the '77 student protests was the occupation of the University of Palermo in December '76, followed in February '77 by the occupations of the universities of Milan and Rome.[5] The occupied University of Rome was also the stage of the defining event of the '77 Movement: the ill-fated speech by Luciano Lama, head of the Communist workers union organization CGIL.

Following the union leader's refusal to open a dialogue with the students and his demand to the already heated assembly of protesters to cease the occupation and to adhere to the party line, Lama was shouted off the stage and a violent confrontation between students and members of FGCI (the Communist Party youth association) ensued. The inability, or reluctance, of the old left to come to terms with the needs of the new left had been exposed and the Lama affair signaled a war declaration of sorts.

It did not help either that in those days Enrico Berlinguer, secretary of the Communist Party, had defined the growing masses of protesters as "poveri untorelli."[6] The protest soon spread to Bologna where it saw its most dramatic moments. On March 11th, following a scuffle between students of the Catholic association, Comunione e Liberazione, and members of the Movement, the college dean asked for the intervention of the police—Franceso Lo Russo, a student belonging to the Lotta Continua group, was shot to death as he was running away from the police.

Two days later, to quiet the protests that had transformed the city into a battlefield, the Communist mayor of Bologna, Zangheri, decided to send in special police forces replete with tanks to guard key points of the city. The *red* city of Bologna, "the city with the most freedom in the world" (according to an unfortunate campaign slogan devised by Zangheri himself), had now been made by its administration into what looked like a sad replica of the events of Hungary and Prague.

A few months after, Bologna also became the stage of the most important meeting of the Movement: the Convention on Repression held at the local sports arena (a concession officially made by the city administration as an act of pacification) in May '77. The meeting was attended by more than 100,000 people from all over Italy as well as by many French intellectuals and students who had carefully followed the development of the protests.[7]

Its great affluence notwithstanding, the convention immediately revealed a split already inside the Movement. On one side, the area of Autonomia was pushing for a more active and violent approach to political engagement; the other, creative side of the movement, although multifarious and fragmented, insisted on a substantially spontaneous and anarchic attitude. Although these two souls of the Movement coexisted for some time, it is undoubtedly the latter that took over in Bologna, thus providing the longer-lasting fruits of the '77 generation.

The profound changes in the composition of society that Italy witnessed in the latter half of the '70s corresponded to the development of an entirely novel phenomenon, that of alternative communication. From this moment on, albeit for a brief period, the use of media ceased to be a privilege solely accessible to the elite. Since 1975, dozens of new, independent, small publishing houses and alternative journals had flourished.

Founded in 1970, the precursor *Re Nudo* "Naked King" (its title a reference to the fairy tale *The Emperor's New Clothes*) had been one of the earliest and most influential of these publications. *Re Nudo* dealt with political and social issues, alternative music, and youth culture. It also published comics inspired by the American underground movement and introduced that ironic discourse that would later characterize the Movement. By 1975, *Re Nudo* appeared almost as a mainstream magazine sold in bookstores and newsstands, but the majority of the *fogli* "sheets" of the Movement of '77 were hand-distributed at shows, squats, and political gatherings and were often composed of two or three pages stapled together.

Among the most influential of these publications in the '76–'78 period were *A/traverso*, *Wow*, *Zut*, *Bi/lot*, *La rivoluzione*, *Viola*, and *Foeminik*. Some of these publications even hosted young comic book artists—Stefano Tamburini, for example, made his debut in the journal *Combinazioni*; and early in his career Andrea Pazienza contributed to publications sponsored by the area of *Autonomia*. This burst of independent publishing was first made possible by the introduction in Italy of offset printing machines—the same phenomenon that jumpstarted the American underground movement in '68—a technique that allowed decent quality at minimal cost. Later, with the arrival of the much more practical photocopy machine, virtually anyone who wanted to publish his own sheet was able to do so. But at the same time, it was the new political climate, the independence from small parties and hierarchies, and the stress on personal action that encouraged and made possible individual publishing initiatives.

Although the "sheets" of these years were very diverse, unifying traits undoubtedly exist: the predominant use of irony and self-referential irony—a feature clearly absent in the '68 movement—and the employment of a new language characterized by a multiplicity of levels from literary to colloquial Italian, from urban slang to dialects. The following excerpt demonstrates an example of irony at work from the pages of *La Rivoluzione* (1977):

> Working makes you free (and beautiful): Millions and millions of young people, due to the present economical situation, are facing the risk of not being able to enjoy that fundamental right/duty that is guaranteed by the Constitution to all the citizens that own nothing else but their own chains: contractual work. As a result, whole generations will miss the incentive for waking up before sunrise, one of the healthiest and most vital traditions in our system. Secondly, the regularity and good spirits that characterize the existence of the honest worker will make way to confusion, angst, deviance. (Echaurren, 29)

The irony is evident, but it might not have been immediately so if this extract had appeared in one of the official journals or flyers of the '68 movement. There is no question about the extent of the gap that had formed between the official left, which was asking for employment for everybody and whose icon and referent was a blatantly idealized and vaguely Rousseauian proletarian/factory worker (a model still viable in the immediate post-war years but totally incongruous in post-economic boom Italy), and the Movement whose slogans were "work less, work more slowly[8]" and "zero work—whole pay check." Rejecting the Communist Party's premise in which the issue of factory work stood at the center of the political identity of the left, "the '77 movement explicitly and consciously presented itself as a movement against factory and salaried work in general, prospecting a progressive decadence of its historical and productive value." (Berardi, 22)

A further unifying trait of the publications of the '77 Movement was the abundance of references to Dadaism (many activists of the Movement proclaimed themselves *Mao-Dadaists*) and to the historical avant-gardes in general. Most notably, the "sheets" of the Movement betrayed a passion for nonsense, both as a weapon and an investigative tool for a political reality that seemed to repel any effort at strict ideological reduction. The mass media of counterculture was, in other words, incorporating the codes of the avant-gardes. As Eco noted at the time, "The new generations are employing in their daily use the languages—or better the multiplicity of languages—of the avant-gardes" (Eco 1977, in Berardi, 65). These codes taken out of their historical context were dealt with in an extra-aesthetic fashion, as pure instruments of day-to-day communication.

One of the Movement's main strategies of counter-information, first developed by Franco Berardi in the pages of *A/traverso* and during his involvement with the independent Radio Alice, then furthered by adult comic magazines such as *Il Male*, *Cannibale*, and *Frigidaire*, was based on the principle that false information would produce real events:

> Counter information denounced the lies of the institutions; wherever the mirror of the language of power deformed reality counter information re-established the truth, albeit as a mere reflection (. . .) Now we need to proceed further: it is not enough to expose the lies of the institutional power, we need to tear apart its truths. When the institutions tell the truth presenting it as the natural order of things we need to expose how inhuman and absurd is the order of reality that the order of their discourse reflects, reproduces, and consolidates. It is necessary to take the place of the institutions, to speak with their voice, to produce signs with the voice and the tone of the institutions. Fake signs. Let's produce fake information revealing what the institutions are hiding. Let's reproduce the magic trick of falsifying truth to say with the language of mass-media what they are themselves trying to avert (. . .) Reality transforms language. Language can transform reality. (Berardi, *A/traverso*, 1976 in Echaurren, 11)

The new adult comics followed this path with great ease because they already intimately reflected and played off this schizophrenic relationship between form (comics institutionally belonging to the area of youth-oriented mass media and therefore employing their languages) and content. The fake front pages of *Il Male* constitute a prime example of this practice of mystification and appropriation of languages: a practice that, once removed from explicit political agendas and repositioned in the field of aesthetics, would lead the artists of the *Frigidaire* group to the contamination with the languages of the avant-gardes and neo-avant-gardes that would characterize most of their best work in the early '80s.

One last common trait of the sheets of the Movement concerned the organization of their graphics. The pages of publications such as *A/ traverso*, *La rivoluzione*, and *Zut* were composed of numerous collages; some articles were hand-written, some in print employing fonts of varying size; and some were designed to be read part horizontally and part vertically. The photographs were all reproduced with a high contrast of blacks and whites, often assembled into montages of disparate elements emphasizing and mirroring the ambiguities and the ironic discourse of the texts. The general look of these sheets—common also to the punk rock flyers and fanzines that will soon follow—closely resembled the freedom and chaotic organization that characterized the publications of the historical avant-gardes, especially those of Dada and Futurism.

This fragmentist, modernist graphic style implicitly linked the Movement with the progress-oriented credo of the historical avant-gardes. The poetics of the fragment suggested faith in the possibility of reconstruction from the ruins and rubbles of the old world, and its employment by the Movement's press betrayed an initial faith in a factual revolution at hand. By '79, the hopes of the Movement having been frustrated, the relationship with the old avant-gardes became less instinctive and more mediated, as the graphics of adult comic magazines showed since the early '80s.

· · ·

Parallel to the expansion of the independent press—and of equal, if not greater, impact—was that of the private radios. Since its inception, television and radio broadcasting in Italy was controlled by the State. For years, Italian audiences had only two state-owned TV channels to choose from: RAI 1 and RAI 2 (a third RAI channel was added in the late '70s) and two State-owned radio stations. Being State-owned, the TV and radio stations were divided among the most powerful political parties.

In the '70s, for example, RAI 1 was, as it had been since the '50s, under the influence of the majority party, the Christian Democrats; RAI 2 was under the control of the Socialist Party; and the newest and smallest, RAI 3, was under the Communist Party. This all changed drastically in 1976 when the Constitutional Court legalized private broadcasting. As a result, in the space of a few months an intricate jungle of independent radio stations and privately owned TV stations began broadcasting locally—there were regional stations, city stations, and even some that could only cover a few neighborhoods.

The Movement jumped on the inexpensive medium of radio and made it one of its most lively and effective means of propaganda. Among the most notorious of the antagonistic private radios of the time were Radio Città Futura and Radio Popolare in Milan, Controradio in Florence, and Radio Alice in Bologna. The diffusion of independent activist radios totally free from the control of political parties and even extra-parliamentary groups had a significant impact on the Movement. It was the first time that the youth Movement had in its hands such a popular and "fast"— in comparison to the press—medium. Now the world of counterculture could, potentially, enter any household.

By far the most groundbreaking of the alternative radios of the time was Radio Alice, which, having sprung from the collective group behind the publication *A/traverso*, began broadcasting in February 1976. The immediate reference of the name of the radio was to Lewis Carroll's character, but it also hinted at Gilles Deleuze's *The Logic of Meaning*, which employs the paradoxes of Carroll's narrative as metaphors of the processes of loss of identity (Gruber, 57). Filippo Scòzzari, an early collaborator of the radio station, remembers it as follows:

> In the Italy of those times, which was just as bad as the present day, the idea of starting a radio station without going through the process of requesting the necessary permits, was considered a scandalous idea in and of itself, and no matter what you would say through those microphones you were held as a criminal. Among the Italian antagonist radios of the times, along with Radio Città Futura, a special mention for its contents goes to Radio Alice a radio whose name is tied to the days of unrest and barricades in the Bologna of '77, and I guess this is why it is still wrongly remembered as a *guerrilla* radio. At the time the number one enemy of the independent radios was the Communist Party—which in fact disappeared shortly after—because it interpreted this explosion of free communication as a way of opening the door to the enemy. Since the Party was mostly concerned with unitary questions the blooming of thousands of radio flowers was no less than blasphemy for them and as a result they had Bifo (Francesco Berardi) arrested and had the police go after the collaborators of Radio Alice. It was hell. It was a mental and political regime that was falling apart whose keepers had no idea of what was happening and kept on as if their hegemony would last forever.

Judge Persico who was at the head of the Radio Alice dragnet is still at his post. I wonder if he blushes every now and then.

The Communists, always the last to understand reality, were witnessing entire portions of their flock escaping their control, portions that they didn't even know existed (the dreaded escape to the far left, later termed "the comrades who are making a mistake"), a proletarian youth absolutely not inclined to obey them and to whom they lacked the ability to talk. When they saw that they had the audacity to create their own media that's when the repression started. That was in '77. Later on, after the riots, either to make amends or fearing that they shouldn't exaggerate with the "control of the territory" they turned a blind eye to the diffusion of heroin that was literally eating Bologna alive. (Scòzzari 2002, conversation with the author)

Radio Alice adopted a radically new rhetoric of information. The language they coined was composed of quotes from the historic avant-gardes (Dadaism, Surrealism, Futurism), literary references, and a non-stop zigzag between the high and low level of language.[9] This is how Radio Alice introduced itself on the first day of broadcasting:

Radio Alice broadcasts: music, news, gardens in bloom, conversations, inventions, discoveries, recipes, horoscopes, magic potions, love, war bulletins, photographs, messages, massages, *and lies*. (www.radioalice.org/nastri.html, emphasis added)

Live news reports were the norm thanks to listeners' calls, as happened with cartoonist Bonvi's live commentary of the clashes between the police and the Movement in Bologna on March 11, 1977, in which the comic book artist described the events as they happened outside his studio windows on Via Rizzoli. The Radio's willingness to broadcast absolutely unfiltered and uncensored live phone calls (which usually consisted of extemporary political rants, complaints against the city administration and the police, personal stories, Dadaist poetry, improvised music, and sometimes commentary against Radio Alice itself) was the true innovative aspect of the station.

Often, the radio hosts themselves would become the audience for the listeners who were phoning in. Radio Alice was therefore inverting the roles between listening and broadcasting, sabotaging the rigid distinction of subjects and objects of communication sanctioned by the official media. Also broadcast live was the report of the police raid on the radio station itself—complete with background noises of kicked-in doors and smashed equipment—which marked the end of Radio Alice's activity at the end of '77.

Just as it happened for the independent press of the Movement and the new adult comics, the truly revolutionary aspect of Radio Alice and of the other antagonistic free radios rested in the destabilizing effect of a conspicuous clash between medium and contents—in Saussurian terms, between the *langue* of the medium and its *parole*. Up to that point, Radio had been one of the official voices of the state; the same voice, but with a different message, was now talking to its audience. At the beginning of Radio Alice's morning broadcasts, a mellifluous female voice with a background of soothing Indian music would greet the listeners with "an invitation not to get up this morning, to stay in bed with somebody and build musical instruments and war machines." It was the first step toward that *media guerrilla*, a furthering of what Eco called *semiological guerrilla*,[10] the first step "from a critically conscious consumption of the already given and the already said to a critically conscious production." (*A/traverso*, June 1976)

By the end of Radio Alice's lifespan, *Mao-Dadaism* (which by now indicated a mix of nonsense, cultural eclecticism, self-referential irony, and political activism through non-alignment stances) had expanded to all sectors of antagonistic communication and action. Even spontaneous activist groups felt the influence of this irreverent climate of ideological freedom and made unpredictability, irony, and mobility their founding axis.

Among the most active and the most deviant in the Bologna of '77 were the Groups of Mao-Dadaist Action, The Blue Flowers Collective (quoting a novel title by Raymond Queneau, who was a darling of the Movement along with Majakovskij, Deleuze, Debord, and Lewis Carroll), the Wild Bunch, and the Fantozzi[11] Column. This last group would expropriate meals in expensive restaurants, fleeing at the moment the check arrived to the shout of "Never again without a second course," an explicit reference to a notorious clandestine publication of the extreme militant left, *Never Again Without a Rifle*.[12] The wealth of cultural references and languages and the total freedom and irreverence with which these activities were put forth underscored the double soul of the Italian '77. A part of the youth movement distanced itself from traditional political activity, although still being actively *engaged*, and produced *culture*; the other, having disappeared from the public eye and gone entirely into clandestine action, gave birth to the phenomenon of terrorism and armed militant groups.

Along with adult comics, independent alternative music reached a turning point in '77, and, like comics, independent music had as a point of departure the irreverent, individualistic and multilinguistic approach that characterized the most active fringes of the Movement. Between '77 and the mid-'80s the creative exchange between alternative music and adult comics was particularly intense and highly fruitful, so much so that it is hard to understand the solutions adopted by one without analyzing the other.

At the root of the expansion of the independent music scene of the late-'70s in Italy was a phenomenon later, somewhat improperly, termed *punk* rock by the music press. Punk rock, which was born in the mid-'70s in the United States with bands like the New York Dolls and, most notably, the Ramones, had its baptism in Europe in '77 with the band The Sex Pistols. In the context and the tradition of rock music, punk rock demonstrated that music could be self-made by anyone; it was not necessary to be technically proficient or to belong to an elite of initiated musicians in order to come up with a commercially viable product and that one could act politically outside a defined ideological structure.

The "no future" declaration sung by John Lydon was in fact hinting at the demise of avant-gardist stances (because the concept of progress is implicit to any kind of avant-garde, in avant-garde mode the slogan would have instead been "no past"). "No future" therefore stood as a manifesto and at the same time as negation of the manifesto itself. Furthermore, punk rock suggested that not only music itself could be self-made, but also its mode of production and diffusion could bypass the major labels. Many punk bands, particularly the American ones at the time, demonstrated the possibility of turning the strategies of big business against them.

In essence, what punk rock was accomplishing in the field of pop music was not very different from what some fringes of the Movement were realizing in the field of media with the creation of their own publishing houses and the appropriation of instruments like radio—employing their structures but reworking their languages. In Italy, the impact of punk rock was strong, although it was very soon incorporated and left behind. The focal point of diffusion for independent music was Bologna, the city that was also at the heart of the youth revolts of '77 and from which point on witnessed a surprising proliferation of bands.

Of great relevance for the success and expansion of the Bologna scene was the example of *Cramps*, an *ante-litteram* independent record label founded in Milan in the mid-'70s. *Cramps* introduced the Italian audience to the works of contemporary composers John Cage and Sylvano Bussotti, the Fluxus international group of artists, and the works of many British radical improvisers such as Derek Bailey and Evan Parker—and later released works by several local independent bands gravitating around the Movement. Among the many bands hailing from Bologna in those years were Kandeggina Gang, Windopen, Kaos Rock, X-rated, and Luti Chroma. But the three groups with the greatest influence on the Bologna scene were Skiantos, Gaznevada, and Confusional Quartet.

Skiantos, founders of a style they called "demented rock," were by far the most Dada-oriented among their colleagues, especially in their visceral refusal of the concept of "art" (the frequent exchange of eggs, tomatoes, and other objects between performers and audience truly recalled the evenings organized by the original Dadaists in Zurich). Roberto Antoni, the group's leader, had inaugurated the practice of what he called "demented language," a composite of metropolitan slang and dialect characterized verbally by an unorthodox use of syntax and graphically by the substitution of the velar Italian "ch" with the letter "k."

Just one look at the bands, the flyers advertising their shows, or even some of the political sheets of the period would reveal how quickly and deeply Antoni's lexicon had permeated the Movement and youth culture as a whole. Along with the new adult comics, this is one of the few examples of a successful and conscious effort to renovate the literary use of Italian by reviving dialect while filtering it through the new a-geographical language of urban youth.

Antoni is also the author of one of the most interesting literary works focusing on the Bologna of the times, *Le stagioni del rock demenziale*, released by the prestigious publishing house Feltrinelli. In his book, the narrative of which, although chronological, is composed of fragments and cut-ups (identical to the graphics of the record covers, flyers and sheets of the Movement), Antoni compiled an imaginary map of the metropolitan youth groups. The meaning of the Rabelaisian enumeration of this census, beyond the surface of the surrealist humor that pervades the book, resides wholly in the utopian project of a language that would eventually impact reality in the hope that, just as the *A/traverso* collective had theorized, linguistic insubordination would produce a factual revolution. Compared to other more commercially and critically successful works on

FIG. 2.1 Confusional Quartet, *EP.*

the period such as the writings of Pier Vittorio Tondelli or Enrico Palandri's *Boccalone*, Antoni's novel now stands as one of the most precise reflections on the spirit of the times.

Along with Skiantos, the band Gaznevada (originally called Centro d'Urlo Metropolitano, or *Metropolitan Scream Center*) was one of the earliest bands of the new Bologna independent scene. Gaznevada's debut LP is highly revealing of the cultural nomadism of post-'77 underground culture, a trait later ascribed to the post-modern canon. The record cover uses Japanese type characters; the lyrics employ English, French, and Italian (sometimes in the same verse); and the cultural references range from Japanese Toho movies to Raymond Chandler's fiction—his short story "Nevada Gas" providing inspiration for the band's name.

The songs themselves are composed of randomly overlapping layers, a practice that calls to mind TV channel-surfing, William Burroughs's cut-up technique, and even the graphics of the Movement's publications. This layering of heterogeneous materials, the ability to interact while still maintaining a certain distance—through irony—with musical and cultural found objects will be seen again in the comics by Tamburini, Carpinteri, and Scòzzari[13] (it is no coincidence that Gaznevada was often referenced and its members featured as characters in the early comics of Pazienza and Tamburini).

Confusional Quartet was an instrumental band whose aim was the realization of its own brand of Futurist rock. As with Gaznevada, dynamism, a taste for fast montage, and the substantial schizophrenic quality of the arrangements played a fundamental role for Confusional Quartet. Italian TV host Pippo Baudo, Donald Duck, John Cage, the movie *Casablanca*, the voice of the Futurist leader Filippo Marinetti (the cover of their second LP (fig. 2.1) features futurist painter Giacomo Balla's *Flowers*), free jazz, *musique concrete*, and punk rock all coexist in one of the most successful musical manifestos of the Italian high-post-modern. Again, it is not hard to see traces of Confusional Quartet's experiments in some of the most structurally adventurous comic artists of the early '80s such as Corona, Carpinteri, and Mattioli.

The continuous references by these bands to the world of images, and vice versa—that of the new adult comics to music, are not only revealing of a coincidence of intents between the two fields,[14] but it also points to the particular relevance the worlds of images and sound had acquired with regard to the verbal linguistic area by the end of the '70s. Therefore, it makes sense that one of the most important art forms that developed in those years is video art.

Just as the photocopy machine had become central as a tool for the Movement because of its speed and low cost, so did the video in relation to film. By '77, immediacy of production became a central factor because these alternative communicators perceived the reality of a rapid shift in the cultural and social context. Alternative cultural products and information proliferated and, in a short time, just as Antoni had predicted, they indeed ended up consuming their producers.

The history of the new adult comics in Italy starts with *Cannibale* in the spring of '77. The name chosen by Stefano Tamburini was that of Picabia's Dadaist journal *Le Cannibale*, of which only two issues were published (in 1920); to maintain continuity, the first issue of *Cannibale* came out as number three. The magazine appeared with a limited printing distributed by Stampa Alternativa, one of the Movement's small independent publishing houses, with Tamburini and Massimo Mattioli as the only contributors.

Tamburini, not yet in his twenties, began his career drawing strips and short stories for *Combinazioni*, one of the journals of the Movement. The other *cannibale*, Mattioli, was already a professional cartoonist, having published in the French magazine *Pif* and, in Italy, oddly enough, in *Il Giornalino*—printed by the Vatican's own publishing house, Edizioni Paoline. For the Catholic comic magazine, Mattioli—likely lured by the prospect of a steady income—for many years drew the children-oriented adventures of a pink rabbit named Pinky. With the following issue of *Cannibale*, published as issue 4/5/6/7 and released with an intentionally confusing editorial strategy of four different covers,[15] Andrea Pazienza (who at the time appeared on the prestigious pages of *Alter Linus)* and Filippo Scòzzari (also publishing in *Alter Linus*, *Linus*, *il Mago*, and *Re Nudo*) joined the ranks. The last member of the group, Tanino Liberatore, was added in the third issue (incongruously published as issue zero).

In '77 the state of auteur comics clearly reflected a gap between its authors and a fringe of its audience that was rapidly changing, so much so that the most successful among the old magazines was *Alter Alter* (formerly *Alter Linus*), mainly because it published the groundbreaking works of the French authors of *Metal Hurlant*. Crepax's middle class interiors and Pratt's exotic adventures in the Caribbean had become rapidly outdated, distant as they were from the social and political turmoil of the late '70s, and were in fact addressed to what was by now an older generation of readers, that of '68 ("At those times auteur comics were middle class, oriented towards the northern wealthier readers and out-datedly left-wing." Scòzzari 2002, conversation with the author)

In this context, *Cannibale* stood out, thanks to several unique features. Firstly, it was born as an independent magazine and belonged to that explosion of antagonistic and alternative press that, as previously noted, occurred at the dawn of '77. A publishing venture such as *Cannibale* was therefore taking to the extreme that detachment from the general idea of its own medium started by the *fumetti neri* in the '60s: the notion of comics as a form of entertainment aimed mainly at young readers but consumed by a wider audience. *Cannibale* was at the same time part of the system of mass media and an alternative magazine because its format and contents were catering to a well-defined section of the reading audience. For the first time Italy had its own underground comics publication.

In his memoirs, Scòzzari remembers his first encounter with Tamburini, who was selling copies of the first issue of *Cannibale* during a meeting of members of Autonomia Operaia[16] in Milan; the scene closely recalls the image of Robert Crumb selling the first issue of *Zap* in 1968 from a baby stroller on the streets of Haight-Ashbury[17]:

> One evening I went back to the headquarters of *Rosso* [a publication of Autonomia Operaia]. This time there were only angry unemployed workers that were getting ready to leave; I had gotten there too late. At the end of the room I saw a chubby kid, with a smile on, wearing overalls and a shirt, long dark curly hair, and he was holding a pile of magazines with a cute name, *Cannibale*. (Scòzzari, *Prima pagare, poi ricordare*, 64)

The great majority of Italian auteur comics fed on a culture and motifs that were by that time codified by the orthodox left, with all its limits, its canonized saints, and its more or less implicit censorship.[18] *Cannibale*, having been born in the midst of the unrest of '77, had instead opened its doors on a reality that the well-established names of auteur comics couldn't or didn't want to relate to.

None of the authors of the old generation would have dared tackle the taboos put on display by the Cannibale artists: stories were tinged with Dadist nonsense; Pazienza depicted the nearly unspeakable subject of heroin and drug addiction in an even more unheard of manner—as comedy; Scòzzari delved into the artistically, politically and socially controversial topic of homosexuality through the adventures of a gay Triestine fashion designer-turned-space explorer; Tamburini set narrations in a futuristic version of suburban Rome with the fauna of hoods, students, drug addicts, and political dissidents meshing Ridley Scott's *Blade Runner* with Pasolini's *Accattone*. It is evident that the cultural references of the school of auteur comics, the adventure classics such as Stevenson, Cooper, and London; Freudian psychoanalysis; Marxism; French naturalism; and post-war American comics were, for the authors of *Cannibale*, ineffectual as a starting point to describe the reality they were experiencing.

Cannibale had the distinction of documenting—as well as inventing and imposing—a new reality at the *very moment* it was taking shape, and at the same time, while tugging comics toward the side of counterculture, it succeeded in creating a typology of intrinsically popular and urban storytelling. The French authors of *Metal Hurlant* had toyed with this idea but eventually trapped themselves in an attention to form that

FIG. 2.2 *Cannibale*, artwork by Filippo Scòzzari.

led to a sterile calligraphism. The stories in *Cannibale* were cynical, sexually explicit, violent, ironic, and openly unapologetic. From the American underground they derived some graphic intuitions (especially from the works of Greg Irons, Robert Crumb, and Richard Corben), along with the deranged ribaldry of its humor. From the French authors of *Hara Kiri*, *Viper*, and *Fluide Glaciale* they absorbed the irreverent attitude and took it to a new extreme. Refused by the editorial board of *Re Nudo* (but later published by Cannibale), Scòzzari's grotesque cover art that portrayed a deformed child with enormous genitalia (the outcome of the Seveso disaster[19]) asking not to be aborted, is probably the summa of the *Cannibali's* cynical attitude. On a deeper level, it was a clue to the group's urge to comment on and reformulate reality (fig. 2.2).

A further innovation put forth by *Cannibale* dealt strictly with the linguistic area. Beginning in the '40s, the influence comics had on the written language in Italy—specifically in a language as traditionally rigid with respect to dialects and spoken language as Italian is—should not be underestimated. The practice of a fast syntax (generally scant of subordinations), the introduction of onomatopoeias, neologisms, and terms borrowed from foreign languages (especially English) had an influence as a rejuvenating and unifying tool second only to that of radio and television. With *Cannibale* and later examples of adult comics, there was a further step forward—not only did the language of its stories employ dialects and urban slang as a mimetic strategy but there was a particular concern, quite close to Emilio Gadda's plurilinguistic approach, with the mingling of high and low levels of the language.

Scòzzari, master of linguistic hyperbole among the *Cannibali*, played with the clichés of high-literary Italian, and Tamburini adopted the youth jargon of the Roman proletarian slums. And taking things to the extreme, Pazienza literally invented a language (which will be analyzed in detail in the next chapter) superimposing the practice of *demented language* developed by the band Skiantos; the dialect of Puglia and Rome, French, Spanish, English, Latin, deliberate misspellings; and an anarchic inclination for neologisms, therefore realizing what is probably the only example of Finneganian language in the comic book world:

> Hai nakakà! Ciao follikol de strep cloria per es! Apice nos! 'Cetta esto picciol recalo, ca caro ce costa, ca cunsta di crammi ticiassett de puriss. eroin de farmacia! E ca quindi es cusì bon ca di nott pianciamo! E no solo de nott ca no ce la spariam intravena! Sigh! (from "Che cosa succede?" Pazienza, *Cose D'A. Paz*, 6)

And again:

> Es tutto preordinè! Du me chiapa i cristiani, io li atiro, e na volta que son
> arrivè . . . ci inietto 17 crammi nel' occhio! Da quand m'è mort Gina mia
> moglie habeo decis de 'matar tuti i spork drughè. (*ibid.* 9)

After nine issues, in July 1979 *Cannibale* shut down, only to reappear
a few months later under a radically new incarnation as the magazine
Frigidaire.

• • •

Il Male, which began in February 1978, initially as a political satire weekly,
was the most popular of all the new adult comic publications (fig. 2.3). It
was born from the ashes of *I quaderni del sale* and directed by comic artist
Pino Zac who was soon replaced by another cartoonist, Vincino. Formerly
the editor of *L'avventurista*, the political cartoon insert of the newspaper
of the extra parliamentary group Lotta Continua, Vincino brought in artists including Jacopo Fo, son of Nobel prize winning playwright Dario.
Beginning with the third issue, Vincenzo Sparagna, a journalist for the
newspaper *Paese Sera* and future editor of *Frigidaire*, joined the *Il Male*
staff, followed by the crew of *Cannibale* shortly thereafter. In a short
time, this magazine that started with a circulation of 20,000 became a
bestseller:

> The birth and rise to popularity of *Il Male* as a popular revolutionary
> journal based on a raw satire of all the dominant values and conventions
> of the times, deeply modified the relationship between the small inde-
> pendent militant sheets and the official press. *Il Male* was in fact born
> as a collective of comrades, but from the start manifested its ambitious
> goal of invading the sphere of official journalism, interfering with the
> big press, exposing the tricks and lies of vertical information, on a mass
> level. (Sparagna in Mordente, *Stefano Tamburini*, 9)

The novelty of *Il Male* as political satire was the lack of any sort of official political affiliation and its reflection of the independent and icono-
clastic atmosphere that pervaded the Movement. Its second noteworthy
asset was the invention of the so-called "fakes." The first fake was a replica
of the front page of the left-wing progressive newspaper *La Repubblica*
that carried the news that the Italian state "had decided to terminate

FIG. 2.3 *Il Male*, artwork by Tanino Liberatore. Pope John Paul II was often the target of *Il Male*'s ferocious satirical work. The caption at the top of the page reads: "Brazil: leprosy is still a problem," the caption at the bottom reads: "I said, kid no kiss the pope . . . no kiss . . . he kissed, there you go."

itself." This was followed by the fake front page of *La Gazzetta dello Sport*, a daily sports publication with the highest circulation of any paper in Italy, announcing the annulment of the World Cup football match won by Argentina against Italy—the appearance of this fake in Rome generated a riot and a three-hour traffic jam in the center of the city.

Other notable fakes included the replica of the first pages of *Paese Sera*, *La Stampa*, and *Il Giorno* "reporting" the capture of the heads of the terrorist organization Brigate Rosse (according to the article, the boss of the organization was Ugo Tognazzi, a venerable Italian comedian who went along with the joke and let himself be photographed handcuffed and escorted by policemen) and the first page of *L'Unità*, the official newspaper of the Italian Communist Party, whose title read: "Enough with the Christian Democratic Party!" (fig. 2.4). This last fake propelled *Il Male* to a record of 48,000 copies sold.[20] Besides the obvious satirical component at the heart of the fakes stood a meditation on the politics of production and consumption of information. The readers had continued buying the fake *La Gazzetta dello Sport* even when the trick had become evident because reading the news off an official organ such as *La Gazzetta*, although a fake copy created the illusion of altering reality.

On a superficial but poignant level, the fake gave voice and exposed a need. The *fake* of *L'Unità* had even deeper implications because it effectively reflected the feelings of a great percentage of the supporters of the Communist Party who were exasperated by the moderate line taken by the Party since the times of the "compromesso storico" (historic compromise) and that had intensified in the *lead years* of terrorism:

> In that climate of general retreat caused by the spread of terrorism, the so-called National Emergency, thanks to which Berlinguer (secretary of the Communist Party) could finally forget the past and join the great ball along with the worst of our politicians, the fact that somebody had the courage to remind everybody how disgusting the Christian Democratic Party was ended up being a refreshing and consolatory statement. Cacciari, member of the Communist Party and opposed to Berlinguer's line, started going around the party's offices flouncing around our fake *Unità* and using it as a support for his own current. (Scòzzari, *Prima pagare, poi ricordare*, 123)

Another of the notorious fakes produced by *Il Male* was the front page of *Giornale di Sicilia*. This time, *Il Male* also managed to get a prestigious intellectual, Sicilian novelist Leonardo Sciascia, to collaborate and "falsify himself":

Quotidiano / Anno LV / N. 189 (***, ***, ***)   ★ Lunedì 19 settembre 1976 / Lira 200 ...

Numero speciale:
diffondetelo in ogni casa

l'Unità

ORGANO DEL PARTITO COMUNISTA ITALIANO

Berlinguer a Genova davanti a una folla gigantesca:

BASTA CON LA D.C!

Una imponente manifestazione di oltre 7 milioni di persone ha concluso un grandioso Festival dell'Unità. 14 cortei di massa. È tempo di avviare un vasto processo di rinnovamento e di lotta. Ormai logora la politica dei sacrifici propagandata da Luciano Lama. La DC è un partito di malfattori. Forse siamo stati poco attenti ai nuovi stimoli che ci venivano dal movimento dei giovani, delle donne, degli omosessuali. La classe operaia protagonista di una svolta storica. La necessaria rettifica di linea non deve intaccare lo spirito combattivo del partito. Prossimo un grande congresso straordinario

Lo storico discorso di Berlinguer

Hanno sfilato per 28 ore

Cronaca di una giornata memorabile

Restituita ufficialmente la parola a Pietro Ingrao

la tromba d'oro

Mario Pastì

Paolo Spriano

FIG. 2.4 *I Male*. Unknown artist. One of the many "fakes" published by *Il Male*.

We confectioned tens of fake Italian newspapers, including some local ones, and I remember a fake made by Vincino; it was the *Giornale di Sicilia* and it bore this title: "Ciancimino [a politician tied to the Sicilian organized crime who was also major of Palermo and member of the Christian Democratic Party] speaks!" In '79 this meant that the whole Sicilian mafia organization could have been blown apart and that issue of *Il Male* sold like hot cakes until the mafia had all the copies in the newsstands of Palermo seized. We had, in other words, gone beyond satire, which was only the wrapping; the "fake" was the measure of truth of the story. And all this despite satire, which for its own nature depends on truthful communication and it's in and of itself a reaction, a critique to something that is already there. (Sparagna, *Frigidaire* 141–142, October/November 1992, 95)

Just like Berardi theorized on the pages of *A/traverso* and through the microphones of Radio Alice, and as in Antoni's *Le stagioni del rock demenziale*, the underlying intuition was that turning the language and the instruments of official media against themselves and practicing linguistic (or mediatic) insubordination was bound to produce factual results with a destabilizing impact on reality, a strategy that would be further developed by Sparagna and the authors of *Cannibale* in their next editorial enterprise, *Frigidaire*. As Vincino, chief editor of *Il Male*, recalled in a recent book on the life of the magazine:

Making up a "fake" was for us an experiment in creative writing in which at center stage stood our analysis of the media world, of their way of recounting reality. The "fake" became one of the most important moments of our engagement with *Il Male* because we reinvented it as a narrative instrument. (. . .) We would appropriate the newspapers we picked, we studied them, we would rewrite them and adapt them to what we wanted to say. By doing this we managed to interpret and recount the times we were living in. (Vincino, 147)

Il Male reached the apex of its popularity during the kidnapping of the Christian Democrat ex-prime minister Aldo Moro in 1978, by which time the extreme left-wing terrorist group Brigate Rosse had already morphed from one of the many independent political groups into a clandestine militant organization. While its guerrilla acts were at first limited to burning factory owners' and conservative union representatives' cars, they soon graduated to the practice of "gambizzare" (literally, drive-by-shooting aiming at the legs), striking right-wing journalists, judges, and political enemies. By the late '70s, the group's activity escalated to a number of ransomed kidnappings, mainly of industrialists and entrepreneurs, to finance their organization. They also distinguished themselves from the other terrorist groups by the nebulous, military-like, and highly theory-laden rhetoric with which they infused their flyers and admissions of responsibility, which were punctually sent to newspapers and national television.

The kidnapping and killing of Aldo Moro came to be the group's most audacious and bloody coup (five policemen were killed during the action in addition to Moro who was murdered after 53 days of imprisonment) and provoked the most condemnation from the public opinion. Aldo Moro was one of the primary power figures of the Christian Democratic party, generally reputed by his detractors as one of the main causes of political stagnation and stunted economic growth (caused by party corruption and internal power struggles) that characterized Italy in the '60s and '70s. Moro was the true force behind securing the "compromesso storico," the alliance between the Christian Democrats and Communists initially introduced by Communist Party secretary Berlinguer in 1975.

Moro, a soft-spoken, strictly observant Catholic, was also notorious for his Byzantine rhetoric (curiously mirroring that of the terrorists who would execute him); his undecipherable public speeches delivered in *politichese* (political lingo); nonsensical formulations such as the famous "parallel convergences" (between PCI and DC); and the infamous claim that since there was no noteworthy political opposition at the parliament his party would have to provide one by being "its own opposition." Nonetheless, Moro's kidnapping generated a unanimous condemnation from all sides of the political spectrum. As for *Il Male*, it reacted with what is justly one of its most infamous cartoons (fig. 2.5): a picture of Moro (sent by the kidnappers to newspapers), unshaven, in his shirtsleeves, behind him the five star logo of the Red Brigades (Brigate Rosse). The caption added by *Il Male* read: "Excuse me, I usually wear Marzotto" (an ubiquitous ad slogan for a popular fashion designer of the time).

No other satirical publication, even in the climate of rising collective indignation for the terrorist act, would have dared so much. To the echo of scandalized protests that followed the publication of that issue, *Il Male* replied with a flowering of cartoons (fig. 2.6), among which was Pazienza's caricature-ish Moro with a small body, enormous head, and a little tear running down his cheek asking, "Are you really going to shoot me? Can I shave first?" (fig. 2.7).

FIG. 2.5   *Il Male.* This infamous cartoon, employing a picture of Aldo Moro taken by his kidnappers, was published by *Il Male* as a centerfold poster.

FIG. 2.6 *Il Male*. Unknown artist. One of the many cartoons that *Il Male* dedicated to the Aldo Moro kidnapping. In this panel, the balloon reads: "I hope the police are coming soon, they always make me wash the dishes here."

The kidnapping of Moro radically changed the orientation of *Il Male*. The development of the Moro affair ran parallel to the development of the magazine, and I am referring to the impact that it had on some fringes of the Movement that were working towards producing real opinion changes. *Il Male* was the only magazine to overturn that hypocritical sanctification of the figure of Moro operated by official media. (Sparagna in Balestrini, 597)

The commercial success of *Il Male* proved there was a wide, uncharted audience for comics and political strips that, though gravitating left,

FIG. 2.7   *Il Male*. Andrea Pazienza. Pazienza comments on
Aldo Moro's kidnapping.

were completely removed from political affiliation, whether the Party
or the extremist groups. These readers were cynical, ironic, auto-ironic,
alien to the auteur comics readership, and visibly the offspring of the '77
Movement. Finally, in *Il Male* the authors of *Cannibale* had the chance to
talk to a much greater audience than their comic magazine would allow.
However, not all of them took the experience of *Il Male* to heart, as they
were somewhat ill at ease among the other all-around satirists, skeptical
of the expressive possibilities that satire could provide, and more interested in the advantages of the extended narrations allowed by the comic
book form.

Of the *Cannibale* group, Pazienza devoted more attention to the project, realizing, in addition to a handful of longer stories, a mosaic of one-panel shots that displayed his ability to combine Dadaist nonsense and realism—capturing behaviors, languages, and youth cultures and implicitly addressing issues still being slowly processed in sociology and literature. His work for *Il Male* depicted the spread of heroin in urban centers, the life of an increasingly unemployed middle-class youth, the police repression following the events of '77, and the political turns of that turbulent end of the decade. From 1978 on, *Cannibale* became a supplement of *Il Male*, which took care of its distribution and promotion. This arrangement lasted until 1980, when the *Cannibale* group opted out to found the magazine *Frigidaire*.

In the context of the new adult comics, and the independent press in general, *Frigidaire* was by far the most innovative publication of the 1980s. With *Frigidaire*, founding authors Scòzzari, Pazienza, Tamburini, Liberatore, and Mattioli refined and surpassed the aesthetic formulations of *Cannibale*—adult comics finally abandoned the sphere of the underground and its creators attained their idea of exchange between the comics medium, journalism, and high- and popular art that the *Cannibale* group had been working on since '77. Most of all, of the publications emerging from the environment of '77, *Frigidaire* best displayed the entity of the social, cultural, and political changes that marked the beginning of the new decade.

Clearly, the events of '77 heralded the development of the climate of the Italian '80s: the first electoral defeats of the Christian Democrats, the crisis of the Communist Party, the barricades of Bologna, the disaffection of the younger generations towards contractual work and the *grand recits* of political ideologies, and the growing cultural debate on postmodernism and post-modern aesthetics. Nonetheless, two other dates are significant in order to comprehend the fast-paced changes brought about by the Italian '80s. The politically active generation of '77, although ideologically skeptical, was for the most part still hoping and working towards a radical change of society they considered imminent—a proletarian revolution at hand was still in the back of the mind of many activists of the time. 1979 was the year that wiped away the hopes of this generation and clearly showed them that a change for society at large was indeed happening, albeit a change for the worse.

The event that represented a turning point for an already agonizing Movement was, of course, the kidnapping and murder of Aldo Moro by the terrorist group Brigate Rosse. The climate of repression, already strong after the barricades of Bologna and the atmosphere of general unrest in major urban centers, intensified in the months following the kidnapping. Hundreds of activists—the great majority of which had no relation to terrorist activities—found themselves arrested and detained, indefinitely awaiting trial. This climate of repression put into action by the then Minister of Interiors Francesco Cossiga (later to become one of the most controversial presidents of the Italian Republic in the mid-'90s) was a strong blow to an already waning Movement and had lasting repercussions on Italian society and culture:

> The disheartening climate of intellectual reflux that invested Italy at
> the beginning of the '80s and that devastated the arts, the university,
> research, cinema, not to speak of political thought, was caused by the
> cultural butchery enacted by the Christian Democrat-Stalinist state first
> in 1977 and then in 1979 (April, 7, 1979 mass arrests of intellectuals tied to
> the Movement many of which were found innocents after being held for
> five years with no evidence). (Berardi, 23)

Moro's killing mobilized public opinion against the extreme left, causing many activists to rethink their involvement in political action, and—on the opposite side of the political spectrum—led to the first complete electoral defeat of the Christian Democrats in 1982. The decline of the Communist Party and the great internal crisis of the Christian Democrats set in motion by the deep scars and divisions caused by the Moro affair left the doors open for the subsequent electoral victory of the Socialist Party led by Bettino Craxi (Prime Minister from 1983 to 1987, whose aggressive, entrepreneurial style of conducting political affairs foreshadowed the Berlusconi regime of the following decade).

1980, the year of *Frigidaire*'s debut, was also notable as the year in which the Italian debate on postmodernism reached its maturity (the works of philosopher Gianni Vattimo, Italo Calvino's *Se una notte d'inverno un viaggiatore*, Eco's *Il nome della rosa*, and the painters of the trans-avant-garde all belong to this period) and the authors of the new adult comics participated in this climate as peers. The most prominent aspects of the Italian high-post-modern, a period that roughly covers the whole decade, can be summarized as: 1) the crisis of great narratives—already observed in the late '70s—as theorized by Jean-François Lyotard in his *The Postmodern Condition* and motivated in Italy by the crisis of communism and of the socialist program in general; 2) the coming to prominence, philosophically, of anti-rationalist stances derived from the Nietzsche-Heidegger line, exemplified in Italy by thinkers like Vattimo as early as 1979 (*La crisi della ragione*); 3) a tendency toward de-hierarchization of cultural levels. This trend set in motion a diametrically opposite movement, one toward the lower ends of the cultural spectrum for the high arts (Eco's *Name of the Rose* setting on the same stage Aristotle and Arthur Conan Doyle), the other toward the high end for popular media like comics (Carpinteri conjugating futurist Fortunato Depero with Sunday pages' comic strip character Signor Bonaventura).

Before continuing with the analysis of the relationship between the new adult comics and postmodern aesthetics, it would be prudent to start with the self-evident, yet necessary, premise that the notion of postmodernism—an aesthetic (as opposed to postmodern, which is an historical condition)—is by no means, and cannot be, a precise and fixed one. As the waning postmodernist debate itself has amply shown, the tag of postmodernism can be tied to a wide catalogue of heterogeneous stances and doctrines: crisis of great narratives, irrationalism and anti-positivism, post-structuralism and deconstruction, narrative self-consciousness, cultural horizontality, the practice of *pastiche*, the substitution of the empirical world with cultural data, etc.

Pushing this position further, far from referring to a great narrative of the postmodern, it should be noted that in the arts there are different strands of postmodernism—and different effects of the postmodern—for each medium taken into consideration. For example, architecture seemed mostly concerned with anti-rationalism and anti-functionalism, whereas painting was decidedly taken with eclecticism and cultural nomadism. Even chronologically, a strict progression of classic-to-modern-to-postmodern hardly applies to all artistic media, if at all.

In the life of the novel, for example, some set the start of the modernist period in the last decade of the nineteenth century, others in the first decades of the twentieth. A postmodernist stage of the novel (dominated by the topos of self-referentiality) started in America in the '60s, while in Italy the postmodern novel, with few exceptions, would have to wait until the '80s.

Comics literally started at the beginning of the century in their modernist phase (switching to a classical stage in the '40s), while alternative pop music had its modernist phase at the end of the '70s and a postmodern stage only in the '90s. At the turn of the '70s, a singular confluence

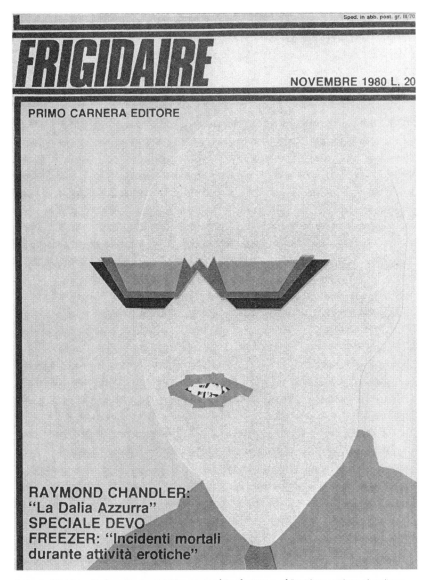

FIG. 2.8 *Frigidaire*. Stefano Tamburini. The cover of the first issue of *Frigidaire*, with its clear lines; sharp, functionalist contours; and glacial tone, signaled a definite cut with the expressionist aesthetics of the underground press and the culture it represented.

of intents in the field of the visual arts appeared in Italy, and the adult comics, especially those from the pages of *Frigidaire*, played a significant role. The *Frigidaire* group not only captured the apex of the slow retreat from political action started at the end of the '70s and managed to talk to a new generation—what has been imprecisely called the post-political generation of the '80s—but they also reflected with great clarity what can be termed the symptoms of the Italian high-post-modernist phase.

The pages of the first issue of *Frigidaire* revealed all those characteristics that the magazine would develop in the following decade. The cover designed by Tamburini (fig. 2.8) presented a *silhouette* composed of angular cut-outs on a bright yellow background, a reference to the geometrical essentiality of the suprematist painters (whose lesson is reflected on the overall graphical project of *Frigidaire*) and at the same time the poetics of the found object; the rigorous composition also hints at the "cold" detached discourse of the magazine and the intention to distance itself from the previous publications of the Movement characterized by an intentionally chaotic, *modernist* design. The contents included an article by William Burroughs, a reportage about the death squads of El Salvador, Tamburini's *Ranxerox*, the scoop of Raymond Chandler's unpublished script for the movie *The Blue Dahlia*, a modern Ovid's *Ars Amandi* with a map-guide to the best gay pick-up spots in Rome, comics by Pazienza and Scòzzari, and an interview with the still-obscure American band Devo.

The comics participated in this cultural-geographical fracturing and they represented its pivotal point—they became information, not by merely chronicling, but by virtue of their ability to synthesize imaginary worlds which were so tightly bound to a reality while being so "other," so undocumented, that they appeared as fiction. In the past, the only field in which comics could aspire to a journalistic function was within the confines of satire (although, as we've seen, *Il Male* had widened its field); with *Frigidaire*, comics somehow succeeded in bringing into view a submerged world and inventing its own journalistic practice.

> One of *Frigidaire*'s challenges was that of coupling comics with reality and reality with comics, almost setting a competition: a cartoonist that needs to duel with reality and reality which needs to produce a show just as captivating as the cartoonist's dreams. To tell the truth us cartoonists would often lose the fight because how can you compete with the reportage on the killer fly or the scoop on Indira Ghandi's assassin? (Scòzzari, 2002, conversation with the author)

But principally, *Frigidaire*'s distinctive quality resided in the choice of a "cold" editorial line, a filter between raw material and its representation that allowed to level between them the *goods* exposed within the pages. There was no more surprise, complicity, or condemnation for the violence in the *Ranxerox* stories or in those of Pazienza's *enfant terribles* than there was in the pictures in the first issue of the magazine showing the massacres in El Salvador or those of victims of S&M practices. The shock value rested in the absence of affection or empathy with the *material* rather than in the object of representation itself. Detachment became the line of coherence allowing the investigation of a world that did not respond to any principle of coherence, to any act of ideological decoding. As Sparagna's editorial from *Frigidaire*'s first issue suggested:

> The idea that we live in a coherent whole, aggravated by the other idea, or better, ideology, that this whole is rational, explicable, continuous, is highly implausible, almost curious. It forces us to be moved, touched, persuading us that we're an integral part, subjects, even protagonists, of events with whom we entertain equivocal relationships. In other words, it prevents us from seeing (. . .). (Sparagna 1980)

In contrast to the Modernist practice, wherein the trauma caused by an active—and therefore still incomplete—process of modernization results in a fragmentary and painful representation, the poetics expressed here springs out of the awareness of a process that is accomplished and completely exhausted. In this sphere, the necessity of the use of the fragment—Sparagna uses the term *compartment*—is not an imposed and unavoidable condition, but a willingly embraced epistemological strategy. Sparagna's reflections are not very distant from those of Lyotard (*The Postmodern Condition*, 1979) regarding the crisis of *grandes histoires*, all-encompassing rationalizations of reality, in the post-industrial society.

In the context of the Italian cultural and political situation, the choice of graphic style adopted by Tamburini for *Frigidaire* is therefore particularly relevant. Whereas the creative fringe of the Movement adopted the language of Dada and the practice of *collage* (be it verbal, visual or cultural), the graphics of *Frigidaire*, embracing "Mondrian rather than Kandinsky" (Sparagna, 1992), signaled the definitive discarding of the Modernism of the second half of the '70s and the fact that a multitude of languages had become available without the necessity of sharing their intrinsic ideologies or teleological instances.

Along these lines, it is easy to understand the reciprocal sympathy between the *Frigidaire* group and exponents of high-culture such as painter Mario Schifano, contemporary composer Sylvano Bussotti, and art critic Achille Bonito Oliva, heralder of the trans-avant-garde. *Frigidare* shared a common ground with the poetics of the trans-avant-garde in particular. Painters like Sandro Chia, Francesco Clemente, Enzo Cucchi, and Mimmo Paladino, under the wing of art critic Achille Bonito Oliva, rediscovered figurative and narrative painting, mixing it with German expressionism, futurism, Dada, and pop-hyperrealism. In the words of Bonito Oliva: "To be an artist now means to have everything available in front of oneself as in a spatial synchronicity" (Bonito Oliva, 6)—a position instinctively shared by the *Frigidaire* artists.

Given these premises, the comics of *Frigidaire* engaged in a confrontation with a historical and cultural reality that had become an objectified fragmentary matter and could consequently be reassembled in an Erector Set fashion. Therefore, it makes sense that the protagonists of their stories are Fascist-era pugilist Primo Carnera, Fritz Lang, teenage hoods, *studelinquenti* (a neologism coined by Scòzzari indicating student activists turned to crime), telepathic art critics, suburban androids, Pablo Picasso, Enzo Ferrari, drug dealers, fashion designers, scientist Antonino Zichichi, and Gabriele D'Annunzio.

The languages of the historical avant-gardes are decontextualized and become mere instruments of discourse. Historical parameters are flattened-out just like the barriers that divided popular art from that of art catalogues and galleries. And so, Bonito Oliva featured in the pages of *Frigidaire* and penned an introduction for a book of collected works by Scòzzari; Liberatore drew illustrations for extracts of Garcia Marquez's *Chronicle of a Death Foretold* that were published as an Italian exclusive in *Frigidaire*; Mario Schifano's Polaroid paintings appeared side-by-side with Tamburini's graphics; Cadelo provided illustrations for unpublished short stories by Boris Vian (an author still largely untranslated In Italy at the time); Bussotti wrote the introductory notes for Liberatore and Tamburini's book *Ranxerox*; the intuitions of futurists Boccioni, Prampolini, and Depero were revisited in Carpinteri's comics; and Scòzzari, with his comic book adaptation of *Il mar delle blatte*, introduced the by-then forgotten works of novelist Tommaso Landolfi to a new generation:

> There was a hunger for models that did not necessarily belong to our specific field of comic book artists. We found out, almost immediately, that

authors were often just as interesting as their works. We went hunting in the world of the visual arts, of scientific research, of literature, searching for those who appeared to us to be bad boys/models. Schifano was certainly one, and so were Bonito Oliva, Kantor, and Kazuo Ohno. We opened our field to avant-garde theatre, the Russian authors discovered by Sparagna, the outer fringes of contemporary music. We wanted to show our readers that there was a totally uncharted and important universe out there and that had never appeared on the newsstands.

The crime that *Frigidaire* was accused of was that of being a popular magazine that had dared enter in official spheres that would normally not be of its competence. One example was the scandal we caused when, regarding the question of atomic cold fusion, *Frigidaire* dared to confront, on a condition of parity, the galaxy of scientific journals. It took us thirty seconds to realize that also in that world there existed a small universe of cheaters, clowns, flakes, geniuses, imbeciles, and heroes. A reality jealously guarded by the watchdogs of official scientific journalism. (Scòzzari, 2002, conversation with the author)

Never before had comics embraced such a wide field, and never before had their authors allowed their creations to graze so freely and impudently in the pastures of literature, science, journalism, and visual arts. This wealth of references and intertextual quotes notwithstanding, the comics published in *Frigidaire* remained eminently narrative. Massimo Mattioli, for example, employed a constant and self-conscious derailment impacting the discourse of his narratives. His puppet-like drawing style clashed against the adult contents of his stories, the organization of his pages changed rapidly from the rigorous grids *à la* Hergé to totally free compositions, and he often employed "outside" materials such as newspaper ads, TV shows, LP covers, found objects, and fake found objects. In a way, Mattioli repossesses everything that Pop Art had stolen from comics and mass media in general to build work that is, in the end, essentially narrative.

In other words, if Lichtenstein employed comics to make his paintings, Mattioli and other *Frigidaire* artists ideally used Lichtensteins to make their comics. That movement of appropriation from lowbrow to highbrow that began in the '60s was turned around and repositioned in that no-man's-land of cultural hierarchies that defined the post-modern '80s. In the same vein, the quoting of Futurist practices in Carpinteri's comics and the formal hyperrealism of Liberatore translates back into mimetic strategies once it becomes a tool of the narrative practice of visual storytelling.

In a wider context, this return to narrative concerns, observed in the painters of the trans-avant-garde, marks a step forward in relation to the literary anti-narratives of neo-avantgardist writers such as early Luigi Malerba, Giorgio Manganelli, and Edoardo Sanguineti and anticipates the Italian minimalist writers of the late '90s. It is no coincidence that the most notorious of the Italian minimalist groups of narrators of the '90s called themselves *Cannibali*. The detached, ironic, highly intertextual narratives of writers such as Aldo Nove, Niccolò Ammaniti, and Tiziano Scarpa clearly revealed the debt toward the authors of the *Frigidaire* group.

In fact, for those scholars looking for the connecting link between the Italian neo-avant-garde and the narrative experiences of the '90s, an argument could be made that the adult comics of the '80s represent just that submerged connecting instance. Notably, the intuitions of Pazienza, Scòzzari, and Tamburini left a mark in the works of the Cannibali narrators, not only in regard to narrative tone, but also in the use of a language that equally employs urban slang, dialects, and mass media lingo, as well as literary suggestions. Recently, a renewed attention for the generation of '77 has opened the way to two movies on the period and the comic artists who documented it: *Paz* (2002) a movie inspired by Andrea Pazienza's comics and *Lavorare con lentezza* (2004), a fiction/documentary on the days of Radio Alice featuring a cameo by a Scòzzari-inspired character.

The golden age of *Frigidaire* lasted approximately five years, although the magazine continued publication well into the '90s and briefly resurfaced in 2001. Stefano Tamburini died in 1986, followed two years later by Pazienza: both victims of heroin overdose and both barely in their thirties. Although Sparagna and Scòzzari continued to concentrate their energies on the magazine, the new generation of authors failed to establish a poetics as incisive as that of their predecessors.

> The authors of *Frigidaire* left their mark on a generation of readers, but they failed in passing a torch which was, after all, impossible to be passed on. In fact, that was never one of our goals. As a matter of fact, no one managed to use *Frigidaire* as a starting point. *Frigidaire*'s research will possibly need the space of two or three generations to be metabolized and reinvented under different shapes. Who knows if I am exaggerating? (Scòzzari, 2002, conversation with the author)

While the *Cannibale* group represented a sharp cut with the previous generation of adult comics, beginning in 1977 a new group of authors made themselves known in the pages of *Linus*, the magazine that had championed the old auteur comics. Whereas the *Cannibali* had as their background the contents and formal innovations of the American underground comics, this second group felt the strong influence both of the adult French comics and some of the Argentinian auteurs such as Alberto Breccia, Muñoz, and Sampayo. In 1980 many of these authors gathered under the banner of a collective called Storiestrisce. Their debut as a group was the series *In fondo è metro* published by Linus in 1981. At that point the group included Igort, Mattotti, Elfo, Bertotti, Kramsky, Jori, and Carpinteri (these last two were also active in *Frigidaire*). In 1983 many of the same artists formed the group Valvoline and their stories appeared in *Alter*.

Compared to the Cannibali, the Storiestrisce/Valvoline collective maintained a moderate line was not too far removed from the editorial policies of *Linus* and *Alter*. There are references to American *noir* in the works of Igort and Elfo, as well as incursions in the world of painting as seen in the Mattotti and Jori's stories, the latter of whom was also respected in the world of art galleries—a double identity/status many of the new adult comic artists aspired to but could rarely attain.

The Valvoline group left many interesting ideas and formal innovations: the montage techniques of Mattotti's early work, Giacon's futurist suggestions, and Cadelo's revolutionary style suspended between hyperrealism and expressionism. Also to the credit of Valvoline was the fruitful exchange with other artistic areas: Igort's involvements, both as artist and performer, with members of the Confusional Quartet; the group's collaboration with the fashion magazine *Vanity*; the video works realized by Elfo, Giacon, and Pozzo for Italian national TV; and the graffiti ads realized in Basel for the Swatch firm. Additionally, Cadelo and Mattiotti (along with Liberatore) are among the few Italian comic artists whose work has been successfully published outside Italy (especially in France and the United States). The Valvoline group, in addition to opening an important school of comics in 1983, *Zio Feininger*, also published its own magazine, *La Dolce Vita*, between 1987 and 1989.

CHAPTER THREE

The Authors

ANDREA PAZIENZA

Pazienza is without doubt the most renowned among the authors of the new Italian comics. Barely in his 20s, Pazienza had already been published in the era's most important comic magazines including *Cannibale*, *Il Male*, *Frigidaire*, *Linus*, *Alter*, *Corto Maltese*, and *Comic Art*. Unfortunately, as is often the case with artists, Pazienza's widest audience and greatest critical acclaim arrived posthumously, following his premature death at 33. As a result, Pazienza is one of the few comic artists of the '70s and '80s whose work has been entirely reprinted and collected in books—even by prestigious literary publishers such as Einaudi—ensuring its availability outside the circuit of specialized bookstores and collectors. His popularity continued growing during the '90s, and a commercially successful (if somewhat tame) movie adaptation of his most popular stories, *Paz*, was released in 2001.

Approaching an exegesis of Pazienza's works means confronting an artistic body of considerable entity—surprisingly so—if one considers that his presence in the publishing industry spanned barely a decade. An artist gifted with a sharp sense of humor but also able to center his poetics on the little horrors of daily life, in the course of his brief career Pazienza tried his hand at autobiography, political satire, adventure stories, comic book journalism, and urban narratives. His knack for combining comedy with tragedy, Dadaist suggestions, and journalistic approach was already evident in his first book-length work, *Pentothal*, a narrative set amidst the

'77 Bologna riots where the hallucinatory quality of the narration blends effortlessly with the all-too-real historical background. This ability to idiosyncratically filter fiction and reportage is, besides the obvious impact of its graphical innovations, in the end the great achievement of Pazienza's work: the formulation of a late twentieth-century naturalism that manages to avoid the seduction and clichés of a neorealist approach.

While still a student at Bologna's DAMS[1], Pazienza published "Armi," his first comic in the magazine *Alter*. A brief story introduced by a quote by Tristan Tzara, Armi's only characters were guns and rifles. In 1977 in the pages of the same magazine, he began publishing the first installments of *Pentothal*, an engagement that Pazienza kept until 1980. From its very first pages, *Pentothal* distinguished itself as a radically innovative effort in Italian adult comics. Firstly, it was an autobiographical narrative with Pazienza himself as the main character: a DAMS student and cartoon artist, occasionally transfigured into his counterpart, Pentothal (the name an obvious reference to the truth serum *sodium pentothal*).

The autobiographical approach was an absolute novelty in the Italian comics canon, and its only antecedents were found in the context of the American underground, namely the works of Robert Crumb and, later, Justin Green. Furthermore, by setting his narrative in the Bologna of '77, the epicenter of the Movement, Pazienza introduced two additional innovations to the comics medium: a precise contemporary historical background and a journalistic approach. Month after month, with each episode Pazienza documented the events surrounding the Bologna Movement firsthand and almost in real-time, so that—for the first time—comics became a source of information on current events.

Pentothal's initial episodes portrayed the violent clashes between students and the police, the arrival of the tanks employed by the city administration to sedate the tumults, the city university takeover, the student assemblies, the long lines at the college cafeterias, the introduction of heroin[2] on the scene (which in a few years would claim the lives of both Pazienza and Tamburini), and even Radio Alice announcing the killing of student activist Lo Russo by the police.[3] Lo Russo's death occurred just a few days after the story originals for the first installment had been delivered to *Alter* for publication. Upon hearing of Russo's death, Pazienza quickly substituted the last page in order to include the breaking news, and he personally delivered the new page right before the magazine's issue went to press (in much the same manner a newspaper editor would deliver a last-minute news item to be inserted on page one).

However, this documentary component is undermined by Pazienza's attitude toward his own narration: *Pentothal* is in fact the first comic of a considerable length (127 pages) to employ the stream-of-consciousness technique. An internally focalized narrative, *Pentothal* progresses despite its lack of a traditional plot by means of an *écriture automatique* that suggests oneiric and irrational solutions. Under this light, it is possible to regard Pazienza's *opera prima* as a repositioning in a popular culture context of the poetics of neoavantgardists Sanguineti, whose novel *Capriccio Italiano* similarly employed the dream-state as an epistemological device, and Nanni Balestrini and Luigi Malerba, authors of stream-of-consciousness, collage-like narratives.

Further complicating his journalist approach, on an intra-diegetic level, Pazienza chose to narrate the Bologna of '77 and the post-'77 years through the eyes of a detached character, an ubiquitous witness who is nevertheless positioned on the margins of the historical events he describes. Employing the picaresque element as a narrative device allowed Pazienza an external point of view in regard to his subject, favoring an effect of estrangement. As a *picaro*, Pentothal is very much a character of his times, suspicious of ideologies and political associations, progressively isolated, culturally omnivorous, and socially transversal. The times of militant political engagement are portrayed as a distant and vaguely embarrassing reverberation, as Pentothal himself muses during one of the many reveries that constitute the narrative:

Vladimiro was at the time the leader of the Marxist-Leninists of Pescara and I was a buddy of "Servire il Popolo." When I told him about my recent sympathies for the Radical Party he was totally unfazed. That's how I realized the total lack of esteem he had for me as a comrade. I thought about it and came to the conclusion that in the periodic act of sticking red stamps on my party membership card there was in fact a spirit akin to that of the Mickey Mouse Club member who aspires to become governor. (44)

Pentothal is then a real-time meditation on the sudden cooling-off of a generation (or sections of it). This *deep-freeze* strategy as a way into the heart of the objects of representation—never translating into narrative coyness, but instead into a sort of strip-tease of the emotionally superfluous—became in the following years a flag and a narrative strategy for Pazienza and fellow cartoonists such as Scòzzari, Tamburini, and Mattioli.

What's more, in its aim to include all that is possible to be represented of an epoch and a specific cultural situation, *Pentothal* is visibly an effort of encyclopediation, almost in a medieval sense. Accordingly, in its dense pages there appear, along the lines of the counterculture of the time, Dadaist quotes; R.D. Laing; William Burroughs; popular and alternative music (Frank Zappa, the Residents, The Ramones, Gaznevada, etc.); the independent radios; the neighborhood bars of Bologna; Pazienza's real-life roommates, acquaintances and fellow-cartoonists Scòzzari and Tamburini; and American underground comic characters (Shelton's the Freak Brothers, Crumb's Fritz the Cat), all of them occupying an intentionally chaotic progression of *bolgie*, the hellish pits of Dante's *Divine Comedy*.

On the graphic level, *Pentothal* presents two innovative trademarks. The first—closely entwined with narrative matters—concerns the plurality of drawing styles employed by its author. This multiplicity of styles, drawing from the American underground comics, Carl Barks's *Donald Duck*, French innovator Moebius, and Italian artists as disparate as Jacovitti and Magnus, has as its counterpart and complement Pazienza's leanings toward verbal plurilinguism—his ability to mix vernacular and literary Italian, urban slang, neologisms as well as terms borrowed from Spanish, English, and French. On a deeper level, the reason for Pazienza's verbal and graphic plurilinguism revolves around the complex and sudden shifts of narrative modes present in his works. If we take a look at the modal scheme devised by Robert Scholes in his *Structuralism in Literature* (132–133)[4]:

Satire—picaresque—comedy—**history**—sentiment—tragedy—romance

we'll see that the majority of Pazienza's work runs nearly the gamut of possibilities, from satire to tragedy, with only the exception of the extreme right branch: romance. As Pazienza's narrative bounces to the left and to the right of the center of the scheme (history), the graphic rendition accompanies the shifts, from the grotesque images of satire, through the puppet-like style of comedy, to the picture-like naturalism of history, and the superrealism of tragedy:

I literally visualize the question of drawing styles as a long corridor leading to many different rooms, each room has a drawing table and on each table there's a different set of drawing tools. When I need to tell a story I choose the room that is most appropriate for that specific narrative, very often in the course of the same story I have to visit different rooms (Pazienza, 1983, conversation with the author).

. . . instead of an implosion, all signs converging in a single stylistic summa or simply many drawings with shared and identifiable elements of affinity, I opted for an explosion, distributing the quality of the sign along a series of diverging possibilities, intentionally exaggerating these differences. (Pazienza, in *Linus* 12, December 1981, 86)

Within twentieth-century Italian literature, the great forerunner of the plurilinguism of the '70s and '80s is undoubtedly Carlo Emilio Gadda, and it wouldn't be hard to draw a straight line from Gadda, continuing through authors of the '60s and '70s such as Manganelli, Arbasino, and Malerba, and finally arriving at the '80s with Pazienza's *Pentothal*. Furthermore, Pazienza's polymorphous accumulation of styles echoes the poetics of contemporary Italian painters like Chia or Palladino who made eclecticism a central prerogative of their works. *Pentothal* is then deeply embedded in the transversality and schizophrenia of forms that characterized artistic production in those years.

The refusal to be identified with a definite stylistic tag is therefore a symptom of the uneasiness of affiliation—political, artistic, and, even deeper, with one's own poetics—that runs through the arts in the late '70s and '80s. As proof, one need only to consider that the eclipse in the Italian intellectual arena of militant groups of painters, writers, or intellectuals and critics tied to a journal has its apex in the mid-'70s. As a consequence of this disenfranchisement, styles and languages became tools one could freely dispose of, which may be the most visible result of the abandonment of the superstition of the modern that informed the artistic etiology of the late '70s and '80s.

On a more specific graphic level, *Pentothal*'s further innovation was the employment of the single-panel page (fig. 3.1), a technique Pazienza abandoned after the completion of this particular work. The single-panel page harkens back to the early days of cartooning. For example both Wilhelm Busch's *Max und Moritz* (1860s) and Richard F. Outcault's *Yellow Kid* (1890s) used single-panel pages: the first organizing its objects in a chronological narration, the second merely suggesting it. It is interesting to note how often groundbreaking adult comic artists from the late '60s on have referred back to this early (and more adult-oriented) period of comics production. One need only to examine the works of underground

FIG. 3.1 Pazienza, Andrea. *Pentothal*. Compared to the geometrical order of King's *Gasoline Alley*'s Sunday pages, Pazienza's meta-panels configure a modernist explosion of space-time coordinates. In this cubist narrative, the balloons require a traditional left-to-right, top-to-bottom reading, but the action does not.

comic artists like Crumb, Victor Moscoso, and Chris Ware to detect the imprint of George Herriman's *Krazy Kat*, Frank King's *Gasoline Alley*, and Bud Fisher's *Mutt and Jeff*.

One of the most interesting uses of single-panel pages, and an excellent example through which to assess Pazienza's innovation in this particular field, is Frank King's early *Gasoline Alley* Sunday in which he employed a narrative structure wherein different panels formed in their totality a single meta-panel, an expedient he used often in his 1930s output. Read in juxtaposition, the panels related a diachronic narrative with a strict Aristotelian unity of action and setting, but when we read the meta-panel in its entirety, synchronically, the category of space—in relationship to the category of time—and the bird's-eye view perspective acquire relevance over the diachronic narrative. In this fashion, King produced a text that can be both synchronic and diachronic, diegetic and mimetic—a text that reveals, almost like a magician showing to the audience the functioning of one of his tricks, the basic continuity of space and action implied by the juxtaposition of panels.

At the heart of what is only outwardly a graphic gimmick rests an implicit faith in space-time relationship or, more precisely, in the possibility of representing it and playing with it—though without ever bringing it to a point of crisis. Conversely, in *Pentothal*'s single-panel pages we witness a methodical unhinging of the categories of time and space wherein the characters float on a jig-saw puzzle of different time-space units, or where, not only space, but a chronological cause-and-effect reading is also put into question (fig. 3.2). This derailment is further complicated by a sequential reading of contiguous page-panels where the narrative is broken down, rapidly changes focus, and just as suddenly ends (there are four fake "The End" captions throughout the whole text). *Pentothal*'s fragmentism is evidently very much in tune with the modernist tinge that colored the greatest part of the artistic products of the '77 Movement; here, the collapse of the categories of time and space is still registered with a sense of loss and dismay. Nevertheless, throughout its four-year run we see a telling change in *Pentothal*'s discourse: the modernist shock is reabsorbed, the emphasis now rests on the freedom of composition, and on the double coding of possible readings. Historical reality, the background of Bologna and its fauna of students and squatters, has almost disappeared—*Pentothal*'s adventures revealingly end at the point where its narrative enters post-modern territories.

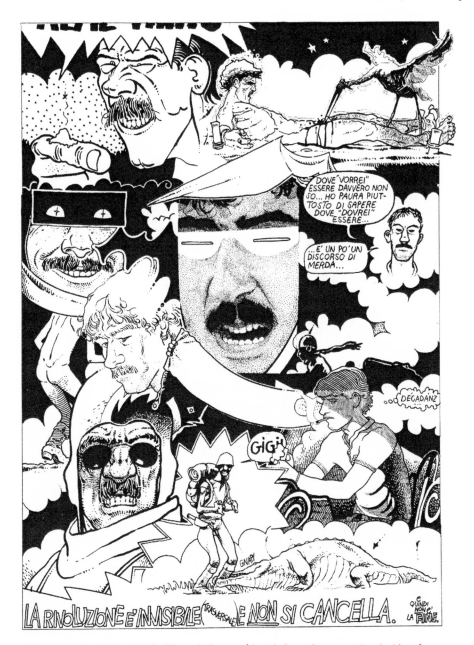

FIG. 3.2. Pazienza, Andrea. *Pentothal*. Through the use of *Pentohal*'s non-linear narrative, the idea of cause-and-effect is increasingly called into question as the result of the collapse of space-time relationships. At the bottom right, one of *Pentothal*'s four fake "End" captions.

Simultaneously with his work for *Alter*, in 1978 Pazienza began contributing to *Cannibale* and *Il Male*. For *Il Male* Pazienza confectioned a great quantity of one-page stories and vignettes that betrayed his taste for nonsense and the Dadaist imprint characterizing the majority of his earlier works (fig. 3.3, 3.4, 3.5). Among the most (in)famous single-panels are those centered on Pope John Paul II and those realized during Aldo Moro's kidnapping.

However, Pazienza's work for *Il Male* can only partly and incidentally be inscribed to the genre of political satire. Once the patina of satire and surrealism is removed, the dominant tone of the output for *Il Male* is intimately naturalistic and has as its subject the languages and culture of the urban youth—that new social subject mentioned in the previous chapter—in all its diverse aspects: the student activists, the culturally disoriented *fuorisede* (non-resident students) from the south, the unemployed factotums, and the underworld of drug-addiction that Pazienza knew firsthand and at which he pitilessly poked fun. Considered as a whole, Pazienza's work for *Il Male* traces a map of the youth culture on the threshold of the new decade and it anticipates, with significant lucidity and greater effectiveness, the work of young Italian narrators of the '80s like Pier Vittorio Tondelli, who attempted a similar analysis through a different medium: the novel.

The impact of Pazienza's strips during his affiliation with *Il Male* can also be strongly felt in the work of the '90s *cannibali* narrators (Nove, Ammaniti, Pinkerle) both in their synthesis of the grotesque of satire and naturalism, and in their employment of urban slang and anti-literary language. Among the long narratives Pazienza published for *Il Male*, *Il Partigiano* (The Partisan) in particular stands out as an exercise of combining light-hearted comedy, satire, and drama. Here, keeping in line with *Il Male*'s agenda of fake information, Pazienza invented a new genre: the faux autobiographical tale, a form Pazienza often returned to.

For *Cannibale*, Pazienza realized a set of short stories which somehow still show strong ties with the American underground of the previous decade. Notably, it is with the *Cannibale* stories that Pazienza begins developing his "pazienzese," an idiolect composed in equal parts of Pugliese, Roman, Neapolitan, and Bolognese dialect; metropolitan slang; neologisms; and occasional English, French, and Spanish terms. In this "Finneganian" multilayering of idioms, it is not hard to identify Pazienza as the last in a long line of practitioners of a *macheronic* debasement of language levels, a tradition started with Folengo and extending through

FIG. 3.3 Pazienza, Andrea. This panel presents Pope John Paul II as seen by Pazienza in this early cartoon for *Il Male*. The balloons read: "What if he really existed? Nah, what am I thinking?"

modern times to the works of Gadda. According to semiotician Omar Calabrese, Pazienza's language has its origins in the spoken language of university students, especially those enrolled in less common fields of study such as sociology, Asian languages, or the semiotics taught at Bologna's DAMS:

> The character of this language is due mostly to the inherent contradiction between university = universality and universe = a rigidly confined

FIG. 3.4 Pazienza, Andrea. The balloon reads: "It was a bad idea on my part to tell you I'm a terrorist, mister. Now you'll tell my father."

world. College is in fact an enclosed environment composed of individuals belonging more or less to the same generation, more or less sharing the same basic culture, and more or less with the same social objectives. Moreover, these people share the same horizons and, to a degree, the same experiences. On the other hand, the world of college is an incredibly open one. If a particular field of study is especially rare, it tends to attract young people coming from different parts of the country, each with their own unique accents, dialects and local cultures (. . .) it follows then that the inhabitants of this world are driven towards a special use of language. In other words, they speak producing signs that will identify them as belonging to that specific group. On the other hand, their jargon is transitory (coinciding with the time of permanence within the group) and it is constituted by the mix of components that participate in it at a given time.

For Calabrese, this language, a spoken one, is none other than the current incarnation of *lingua volgare*: "the transitory language of a community opposing itself to a traditionally sanctioned one":

Then someone comes along and gives an aesthetic or ethical value to this language by using it for political or artistic ends in order to manifest a sense of identity, a value of freshness or authenticity, or the meaning

FIG. 3.5 Pazienza, Andrea. In this cartoon for *Il Male*, Pazienza, a user himself, makes fun of heroin junkies. However, Pazienza's rendition of this comical return of the prodigal son is so accurate (both verbally and graphically), that the end result is not totally lighthearted. The balloon reads: "Hi mom, hi dad. I am back for good. I am through with fooling, shooting drugs, and bad company. I am back to stay, to eat with you, to ask you for money to go to the movies, to be woken up early every morning, to have you buy me the clothes you choose, along with pressed shirts. Shirts! I want my room back, and new friends, and I want to go to the beach with you, but only if I'm good! Do you remember? It was summer, in the countryside, and you were picking cherries and putting them around my ears, like earrings . . ."

of the changes of the status quo. This was done by authors who became points of reference in our culture, authors such as Dante, Rabelais, Ruzante, or Chaucer. Every now and then, this also happens to modern authors. It seems to me that Pazienza belongs to the number of these pioneers, these innovators, along with Pasolini and Dario Fo. (Calabrese, in Paganelli 1991, 12–15)

As noted in the last chapter, Pazienza's fractioning of linguistic instances (in a broad sense: purely verbal, visual, even aural) is very much embedded in the *modernist weltanschauung* of the '77 Movement and we can find examples of it in the collage-like quality of the montage of many of the compositions of the bands in the Bolognese underground scene, in the multilayered graphics of the alternative publications, and even in the mix of high- and low-levels of language employed by antagonist media (Radio Alice, the sheets of the Movement). The year 1980 is nonetheless a watershed, both politically and culturally, and Pazienza's work reflects these changes faithfully. Having reabsorbed the modernist fragmentation and exhausted the experiences with *Pentothal*, *Il Male*, and *Cannibale* at approximately the same time, Pazienza started his work with *Frigidaire*, producing his most mature works and inaugurating the *Zanardi* cycle that debuted in the fifth issue of the magazine.

As an introduction to the *Zanardi* stories, Pazienza published the story *Giorno* in *Frigidaire*'s third issue. In short, *Giorno* contains all the elements that became signatures of Pazienza's work: the great attention to the organization of the diegetic elements, the strong naturalist suggestions, the Bolognese setting, and a tighter control and economy of graphic-stylistic means. The narration, by means of alternate montage, follows the day of three characters from 7:35 a.m. to 4:45 p.m. (between dawn and dusk) of the 25th of November.

The first character, Sergio, is led to believe by his girlfriend that she betrayed him and he is now on the trail of the other man. Enrico Fiabeschi, a college student, must take a cinema exam, the results of which will determine his eligibility to avoid being drafted,[5] and on whose subject, Francis Ford Coppola's *Apocalypse Now*, he is totally unprepared. The last character, unnamed, is trying to work up the courage to get rid of three uninvited acquaintances who have occupied his apartment for months. The story of two other characters, a man and a woman who live secluded at home occasionally watching the outside world from their windows, constitutes a framing device that opens and closes the narration ("Hop," says one of the frame characters, "it's night again. Soon it will start raining, then it will stop, it will start again, and tomorrow morning it will stop once more. These are cold and dull days, and we're doing the right thing not going out, staying in bed, in the dark, you and I").

The frame is then a function of the detachment that Pazienza imposes on his narrative as a mimetic strategy, as a guarantee of a further *effet de réel*. Along these lines, the violence and the horrors of the day are de-sensationalized, de-semantized, and offered in their essence in their elementary mechanics. Pazienza's own brand of naturalism is therefore alien to explicit social or historical *great narratives* (in Lyotard's terms), or even to imposing an authorial ideology on the diegesis. Furthermore, if an ideological structure is to be obtained at all from this particular narrative, the two characters of the frame are an incarnation of the retreat to the private that the '80s had opened for many of the protagonists of '77: from engaged activists to detached, if lucid, witnesses.

Nonetheless, Pazienza's great artistry in these stories rests in his ability to suddenly open loopholes in his photographic approach, providing accurately dosed niches of pathos in order to tie together character and reader. For example, one should notice how the subtle gesture of the hand of the character in fig. 3.7 (fourth panel) serves both as a function of characterization and as an empathic link between reader and *persona*, and how immediately afterward a sudden ellipsis cold-heartedly projects the narration to its grotesque climax. But *Giorno* is also a meta-diegetic meditation on the function of signs and on the endless possibilities of semantic surfaces. And it is not by chance that a reference to Baudrillard's *On Seduction* (53–130) appears halfway through the narration, superimposed on the sequence showing Enrico Fiabeschi musing on "that abyss that is the Surface" while choosing his attire—ironic *vestizione* of the hero—for his ill-fated cinema exam (fig. 3.6):

> Superficial vertigo, superficial abyss. Pure appearance: therein lies the space of seduction. Not within signs but within appearances. And this is another basic distinction: an appearance is not a sign. A sign can be de-codified, an appearance cannot. *Power* as a way to master the world of signs is diametrically opposed to *seduction* as a way to master the world of appearances. A sign must abide its laws, appearances don't. The strategy of seduction in its whole consists in making things accessible

FIG. 3.6 Pazienza, Andrea. *Giorno*.

to appearance, to make them shine in their pure appearance, to exhaust them in their appearance, in the game of appearances. (Pazienza, *Zanardi*, 17)

Accordingly, *Giorno* configures itself as an extended parable, taking place on the border between signs as a function of univocal semantic production (the territory of cause-and-effect relationships) and surface of the discourse as dominion of appearances (the realm of seduction). On this borderline *Giorno*'s characters are ultimately defeated. On a diegetic level the attempt of seduction/infraction in Enrico Fiabeschi's exam sequence fails and he is consequently relegated to the normative realm of signs and cause-and-effect categories whose relationships he can't master. The unnamed character's talk with his "roommates" fails as an act of linguistic dissimulation, because his body language involuntarily produces signifiers that invalidate his discourse as an attempt of seduction/deception ("to seduce is to die as reality and reconstitute oneself as illusion [. . .] the strategy of seduction is one of deception." Baudrillard, 69)

Sergio, a victim of seduction (his never-seen girlfriend is the only successful seducer in *Giorno*), is caught in the abyss of appearances and makes a faulty reading of signs, a hermeneutic/deductive mistake that will later bear dramatic consequences. The iconic and linguistic clusters of signs in the story themselves acquire a further semantic plus-value in their redundancy and interact on the surface of the narrative discourse: the metal bar used by Stefano to kill his supposed rival becomes in one of the last panels—at a maximum degree of stylization—a linguistic sign rather than an iconic one (fig. 3.7); the hole in the shoe of the victim as a

FIG. 3.7 Pazienza, Andrea. *Giorno*. The metal bar, one of the recurring icons of the story, is reduced to a linguistic sign in panel five of this page. It is now a dash sign marking an elliptical jump-cut in the narrative. Thus, the violent climax of the two remaining story lines is glossed over. Note also how in the architecture of the page as a whole, the bar appears in panels four, five, and seven, making a straight line that, like a bridge, connects (but also points to) the conclusion of the first story line.

clue, the serpent/river, the central metaphor of Conrad's *Heart of Darkness* and Coppola's *Apocalypse Now*, in which the professor metamorphoses during the exam; and the father/bird figure in Enrico's dream all conjure, escaping a univocal decoding, a parallel narration of sorts in the texture of the diegesis.

This strategy once again implicitly refers to Baudrillard's notion of surface abyss (53–55), that zone of the discourse where signs resist a normative hermeneutical act. In addition, on a structural level, Pazienza meditates on seduction as a metaphor for the graphic sign as a narrative device and, therefore, on the problem of the referential function of graphic icons: what part of an icon translates into a sign and what instead remains subject to the realm of seduction and of the *superficial abysses* that its discourse unlocks.

Both in its Bolognese setting and in its formal and narrative concerns, *Giorno* introduces the *Zanardi* cycle, a series of stories that mark Pazienza's most mature output. The *Zanardi* cycle tells the adventures of three high school students, enfants terribles Zanardi, Colasanti, and Petrilli. The improbability of the plots is evident: in just the first four stories, the teenagers are involved in hold-ups, extortions, blackmail, morphine and heroin dealing, and, to top it all off, they cause the death of the dean of their school and set fire to an all-girls institute. Pazienza's naturalistic project is central here, but on a deeper level than it may seem, and the accuracy of the language, the settings, and the gestures resonate. Zanardi isn't, after all, more real than Superman, but it is the environment that surrounds him and the traits that sum up his character that provide the *effet de réel*. The first story of the cycle, "Giallo Scolastico" (a double entendre between "high school detective story" and "traditional—according to the rules—detective story"[6]), is justly held as the high point of Pazienza's career.

Pazienza reveals himself here as a skillful director with an eye for detail and character, meticulously regulating the rhythm and the montage of the narrative. In the *Zanardi* stories the graphic component becomes thoroughly narrative and the multilayering of styles in relation to earlier works, although still a functional element, is kept under tighter control. The question of the varying levels of abstraction of graphic rendition and its relation to the multiplicity of narrative modes is in this context extremely subtle but central nonetheless.

Pazienza employs an illustrative style that is certainly indebted to Eisner's *Spirit* in its elasticity. The backgrounds of Zanardi's world—the

FIG. 3.8 Pazienza, Andrea. *Giallo Scolastico*. In the first panel, from right to left, are Zanardi, Petrilli, and Colasanti. The anatomical rendition of the three characters here is an explicit function of characterization. Note how Zanardi is transfigured in the third panel. The arrow points down at the girl who is the target of his revenge, suggesting once more the meta-panel construction found in *Pentothal*. As a result, the reader is made aware of the coexistence of fictional space (the intradiegetic space that Zanardi crosses to walk up to the girl) and empirical space (the actual space that panels occupy on the page that the reader has to cross by reading).

suburbs, squares, school buildings, and clubs—are rendered with obvious mimetic intentions and they work as a realistic stage for the characters, all of which are subjected to a different degree of abstraction/deformation. The rendering of the trio, Zanardi, Colasanti, and Petrilli, represent a telling example of this strategy at work (fig. 3.8).

Zanardi, the mastermind and supervisor of the crimes of the trio, is a character that is all surface; impassible and characterized by a clinical, detached cruelty; and serves as the infallible negative hero of the cycle. As such, in the modal scheme discussed above, he occupies the slot of Romance and therefore belongs to the world of *Übermensch* and undefeatable (negative) heroes. Consequently, Pazienza visually translates these qualities into a deformation of anatomical traits, rendering his character with a long slender body and an anti-naturalistic beak-like nose suggesting the image of a predator. In some panels Pazienza deforms Zanardi's

FIG. 3.9 Pazienza, Andrea. *Pacco*. A visual metaphor: In a sudden stylistic shift, recalling the swift metamorphosis found in the Tex Avery and Fleischer Studios cartoons, Zanardi becomes—for the space/duration of a single panel—a rocket.

anatomy to the point of presenting him, per visual synecdoche, in the form of a spear (fig. 3.8, first panel) or a rocket (fig. 3.9).

On the opposite side, Petrilli, a tragicomic (and covertly autobiographical) figure oppressed and defeated by the world he lives in, is represented with curvy and puppet-like features—so where Zanardi's nose is pointy and angular, Petrilli's is round and puffy. This character, given his conflictual stance and his sense of impotence in respect to the fictional world he's thrown into, belongs to both the world of the Comedy and Tragedy.

In the center stands Colasanti, a character capable of crimes just as heinous as those orchestrated by Zanardi but more accessible and provided with an internal life available to the reader. Consequently, he is the

FIG. 3.10 Pazienza, Andrea. *Giallo Scolastico*. A metafictional touch: Colasanti, who has just bought a copy of *Frigidaire* (and thus probably reading his own adventures), says: "Pazienza is really the best, practically a rock star."

FIG. 3.11 Pazienza, Andrea. *Giallo Scolastico*.

character rendered with less abstraction and a higher degree of anatomical correctness: of the three, Colasanti is closest to the History slot. Each text necessarily establishes its own fictional plane of reality through the combination of its own parts, and the anchoring to the History slot provided by Petrilli's character is tied to a notion of reality formulated by the text itself: that level of agreement with the verisimilitude[7] of the narration the reader must accept in order to share in the narrative game.

Pazienza's thoughtfulness as a narrator is revealed here by his lucid distinction between an ephemeral concept of the real and the *effet de réel* where he organizes employing verbal gestures, pop codes (music, fashion), and metropolitan glimpses. He also includes subtle self-referential touches; for example, throughout the middle of the story Colasanti stops by a newspaper stand, buys a copy of *Frigidaire*, and comments on Pazienza's *bravura*. The following panel shows a leather-clad figure, totally extraneous to the story, contorting in a statuary pose (fig. 3.10). This narcissistic aside, a slight demystification of the narrative act, is an authorial wink that maliciously endangers the mimetic/naturalistic project of the story. A further example of metanarrative instances is shown in fig. 3.11 wherein Pazienza again plays with the referential and iconic values of the graphic image, therefore underscoring once more an impish authorial presence: the crossed-out spaghetti dish works here like a symbolic sign rather than an analogical iconic one.

"Giallo scolastico" narrates the adventures of the trio in pursuit of Zanardi's address book, whose cover is stuffed with heroin, and which ended up in the school headmistress's hands. In the end, it turns out that Zanardi had lied about the heroin stashed in the book in order to jumpstart a gratuitous series of criminal domino effects. Thus, it is easy to see in Zanardi a seducer figure, fictional counterpart of the authorial figure who, unlike the characters in "Giorno," is able to effortlessly master the realm of appearances. Around this *canovaccio* Pazienza organizes a taut plot in which his "deep-freeze" poetics translate into a narrative rhetoric that employs distance (as a narrative strategy), ellipsis, and understatement as its cardinal points.

Pazienza authored four more Zanardi stories for *Frigidaire*. Then in the late '80s the character reappeared on the pages of *Comic Art*, a more conventional comics magazine, but by this time both the impact of the Zanardi stories and the verve of their creator were waning. Among Pazienza's later works, the most important, both because of its length and the emotional participation of its author, is the autobiographical *Gli ultimi giorni di Pompeo* (fig. 3.12). The title is another of Pazienza's semiserious double entendres: a reference to the last days of his hero, Pompeo, the name itself a nod to the character's habit of consuming (pumping) heroin, and to Edward George Bulwer-Lytton's historical feuilleton and its popular Italian 1913 film adaptation, *The Last Days of Pompeii*.

FIG. 3.12 Pazienza, Andrea. *Gli ultimi giorni di Pompeo*. The caption reads: "Pompy goes to the restroom to shoot up. It's the sixth time since this morning."

The story was published in monthly installments in *Alter* between 1984 and 1986 and collected in book form in 1987. As the author suggests in the story's closing notes, Pompeo is Pentothal ten years later: gone is the background of the '77 generation, the playful Dadaist suggestions, and the absurdist humor. This older Pentothal reached the mid-'80s as an isolated and tired comic book artist who wanders through a grey and deserted Bologna looking for his heroin fix. *Pompeo* is one of the very few of Pazienza's works where the "cold" mediation between character and narrator gives way to a free-flowing narrative introspection. Even the graphic style employed in *Pompeo* is intentionally stark, characterized as it is by an expressionistic immediacy, whereas in *Pentothal* Pazienza juggled an array of heterogeneous visual solutions. Only the construction of the pages at times recalls the meta-panels employed in *Pentothal*.

As the title suggests, *Pompeo*'s narrative follows the hero throughout the two days preceding his suicide. The narration opens in *medias res* showing Pompeo several minutes before overdosing on heroin; it then flashes back to the previous day, until ultimately the timeline returns to the *incipit* with Pompeo surviving the overdose coma and committing suicide a few hours later. The employment of the *medias res* artifice suggests the author's intention to formulate a contemporary epic tale of sorts, a strategy the text itself self-consciously hints at right from the first splash panel: Pompeo reading a passage from Alessandro Serpieri's book on T.S. Eliot (*Le strutture profonde*, 1974), which is centered on the *Waste Land*'s adoption of myth-derived figures and its management of formal structures.

Compared to *Pentothal*, wherein the text revolved mostly around the seduction of Pazienza's visual inventions and instant associations, *Pompeo* is primarily a narrative text that leaves ample space to the voice of its narrator. Most pages are in fact almost exclusively occupied by text, and the drawings often seem to work as an illustration of the narrator's tale. Interestingly, as Pazienza moves into the autobiographical sphere, he feels the need to differentiate the figure of the character from that of the narrator—indistinguishable in *Pentothal*—and also to throw in a thin disguise between author and character: Pompeo's long bony nose masking an otherwise obvious self-portrait.

Nonetheless, *Pompeo* still retains many of Pazienza's traditional stylistic trademarks: the shifting of graphic stylization from realistic to caricatural, the open-panel organization of the page, and its author's passion for quotes ranging from Daphne du Maurier, Alexander Blok, Boris Pasternak, Vladimir Mayakovsky, and Sergei Yesenin (the latter two, young suicides—just like the protagonist of *Pompeo*), to fellow comic artist Marcello Jori—whose drawing style Pazienza quotes whenever his friend enters the narration. At one hundred and sixteen pages, *Pompeo* stands out as one of the most ambitious and narratively compact examples of the new adult comics and certainly the first *de profundis* in the field of comics as a whole.

As an indication of the dramatic changes that occurred from the dawn of '77 and the mid-'80s, *Pompeo* represents the apex of that inexorable and painful shift from the social to the private sphere whose seeds were already traceable in *Pentothal*. The reading key is therefore neither the naturalistic nor the (obsolete) neorealistic one that many enthusiast reviewers erroneously imposed on Pazienza's last opus, regarding the author as a demiurgic reporter of the '80s youth, a sort of contemporary Pier Paolo Pasolini or, worse, a Tondelli *ante litteram*. The proof is that as a document on contemporary youth *Pompeo*'s narrative revolves exclusively around the consciousness of a protagonist that is by definition removed from the outside world. On an intimate level, *Pompeo* doesn't deal with the specifics of heroin addiction or with the mechanics of the problem as a social one, but in a much subtler and personal fashion reflects the loss of connection with the political—in the broader meaning of the term—that the '77 generation experienced at the onset of the following decade.

If an epic reading is appropriate, as the text structure itself suggests, *Pompeo* deals with a generation, Pazienza's own, caught in a painful process of transition and growing isolation; making *Pompeo* a dystopic epic recounting not the mythical origin of a specific culture, but rather its demise. Accordingly, the topos of a premature aging process appears as a *leitmotif* throughout the entirety of Pazienza's output in the '80s: "Now that I live in the country," wrote Pazienza in the final notes to *Pompeo*, "the young people here call me old *Paz* and, just to let you know, I'm only 29" (125). In this sense, the Pasternak quote which Pazienza included at different times in his later works (including *Pompeo* 94), becomes particularly emblematic: "But old age is a Rome, without tricks or apologies, requiring no proofs from the actor, but a complete indisputable downfall."

The final period of Pazienza's works reveals a certain lack of inspiration and a progressive loss of creativity. Having abandoned the *Frigidaire* collective, Pazienza began publishing in more traditional comic magazines such as *Corto Maltese* and *Comic Art*. Both Pazienza's separation from the *Frigidaire* group with which he had developed artistically and his exposure to a more conventional readership contributed to the sense of displacement revealed by his final works.

His last published story, left unfinished, told the tale of an oversized bulldog employed by Hannibal's Punic army during battles. In the last panel the dog protagonist is seen bowing down to a mysterious opponent, a gigantic black dog coming out of the fog. In 1988 at age 33, Pazienza died of a heroin overdose, leaving a great void in the field of the Italian adult comics. Furthermore, Pazienza not only left an important legacy to his fellow comic artists, but his influence is conspicuously even stronger in the field of literature, mostly so among prominent short story writers of the '90s such as Niccolò Ammaniti, Aldo Nove, and Tiziano Scarpa. To this day, no other Italian comic artist has equaled his narrative talent, his intensity and depth, and his impish ability to let his narratives bounce seamlessly from comedy to tragedy, and chronicle to fiction.

FILIPPO SCÒZZARI

Of all the late '70s Italian adult comic artists, Filippo Scòzzari is undoubtedly the most lucid, the most poetically coherent, and, artistically speaking, the most long-lived. In Scòzzari's remarkable artistic output one can't help but recognize the original sparkle of the irreverent, cold, and idiosyncratically cantankerous poetics that characterized the best examples of the Italian adult comics between the '70s and '80s. His output, like that of his colleagues Tamburini, Pazienza, and Mattioli, reveals not only a marked postmodern taste for quotations, but first and foremost an intention of reformulation of reality that goes far beyond the confines of satire and parody.

Accordingly, the theatre of his works is crowded with grotesque masks and recurring target figures drawn from the pantheon of the Italian cultural-historical collective imagination: boxer, actor, and superstar of the fascist regime, Primo Carnera becomes a Triestine fashion designer and later a metaphysical space traveler; poet Gabriele D'Annunzio, a coprophiliac Brazilian aristocrat; nuclear scientist Zichichi, a futuristic multimillionaire victim of a terminal alien disease. Above all, in Scòzzari's works a conspicuous narrative drive emerges that, while springing out of the acknowledgement of the exhaustion of genres typical of *pastiche* (the science fiction of *Capitan Dulciora*, the noir of *Dalia Azzurra*, the detective story of *Dottor Jack*, etc.), nonetheless sets them into play throughout an ironic rhetoric that reaffirms in the end the need to tell stories.

Unlike the other comic artists of his group, Scòzzari belongs to the previous generation (there was, for example, a ten-year difference between him and Pazienza). Virtually untouched by the events of '68, Scòzzari's ironic verve found its natural humus in the skeptical and unstable climate of '77—and it is no wonder that his recently published autobiography, *Prima pagare poi ricordare*, has its incipit in that same year. The sense of detachment from their own generation that Pazienza and many others of the group were to varying degrees traumatically coming to terms with was therefore a given fact for Scòzzari who, if anything, felt a much greater kinship with the milieu of '77 than with that of '68.

Scòzzari published his first stories in 1976 in the pages of *Il Mago*, one of the many *Linus* knock-offs, and later contributed to the underground magazine *Re Nudo*. In this early period, Scòzzari's style revealed the strong influence of the underground American comic artists, especially Greg Irons and Richard Corben. For *Il Mago* Scòzzari authored two science fiction stories (with a particular adult bias that did not quite match the expectations of the readers of a magazine addressed mostly to pre-teens) and an adaptation of Ambrose Bierce's short story *Oil of Dog*. The American author's dry and venomous humor

FIG. 3.13 Scòzzari, Filippo. *La Dalia Azzurra.*

FIG. 3.14 Scòzzari, Filippo. *Primo Carnera e la gara di squisitezza.* From left to right: Italian prize-fighter Primo Carnera and German director Fritz Lang.

FIG. 3.15   Scòzzari, Filippo. *Che cosa si può ottenere con la macchina del tempo.*

matched seamlessly with Scòzzari's own, but the subject of the story (belonging to Bierce's infamous *Parenticide Club* cycle) provoked so much indignation among readers that it marked Scòzzari's last contribution to the magazine.

One constant throughout Scòzzari's career was the grotesque deformation of the anatomies, particularly the facial features of his characters (figs. 3.13, 3.14, 3.15). This is not merely the influence of the American underground authors of the previous decade, but rather due to a deeply rooted and deliberate narrative strategy. In Scòzzari's works, the narrator (which in the comic *medium* translates both as the narrating voice—when present, and the illustrator responsible for the *mise en scene* and graphic rendition of the story) openly manifests a vibrant dislike for its subjects. Thus, the narrations often develop along the lines of an ironic discourse wherein the communication between author and reader is established above the heads of the characters: a double discourse through which the caustic voice of the authorial figure sabotages and hijacks the coordinates of the diegesis.

The result is a self-conscious split between a straight-faced narrator who diligently tells the story and an ironic author as a function of the text who, lurking behind the curtains, undermines his efforts: a narrative device that in literature has its forerunners in Pulci, Rabelais, Cervantes,

Voltaire, and Fielding, just to name a few, but which was never quite so deliberately employed in comics. Such a narratorial device is present in the adaptation of Raymond Chandler's screenplay for the movie *Blue Dahlia* that Scòzzari serialized in *Frigidaire* from 1980 to 1982.

The *scoop* of Chandler's unpublished screenplay was given as a present to *Frigidaire* by novelist, journalist, and *Linus* editor-in-chief Oreste del Buono. After reading a few pages of Chandler's convoluted plot, Pazienza, who had initially agreed to work on the adaptation, cautiously renounced and passed the job to Scòzzari. Although the encounter between Scòzzari and Chandler happened fortuitously, it is nonetheless meaningful.

While in Chandler's works the *picaro*-hero moves in a degraded and misshapen reality and is therefore the only link between the narrative world and the reader, Scòzzari severs even this last bond. The modernity (or possibly the post-modernity) of Scòzzari's version lies in his willingness to redirect Chandler's substantially bitter irony in the direction of the text itself. Therefore, the sense of Scòzzari's version rests in this constant parartextual shift between adhesion to and infraction of the rules of the *other* text.

Consequently, there is a double narrator: one that diligently tells the story (and is occasionally fascinated by it) and another who—exasperated by it—tries to bring it to a point of collapse. Additionally, the text reveals a double ironic level: the imprint of Chandler's own (whose implicit romanticism clashes with Scòzzari's coordinates), and the one generated by Scòzzari's adaptation which falls, with a deliberate boomerang effect, on the text itself. The postmodern paradigm is easy to see: the "modern" Chandler employs irony in regard to a fictional world, whereas the "postmodern" Scòzzari's turns it towards a literary text. Scòzzari's *La Dalia Azzurra* is therefore not a parody, but an example of *pastiche* (in the definition given by Jameson[8]) generated by the superimposition of two different visions and sensibilities that, in a sort of literary ballet, constantly join and separate.

But there's also a second paratext that plays a relevant role in Scòzzari's adaptation: the movie directed in 1946 by George Marshall, a cinematographic version that Scòzzari maintains he viewed for the first time years after finishing *La Dalia Azzurra*[9] (though, truth be told, the comic book adaptation not only clearly replicated the actors' physiognomies, but also quoted shots and montage devices found in the film version). This helps to explain the cinematographic nuances of Scòzzari's adaptation: the presence of numerous sequences with low levels of ellipsis, the choice of the grey tones alluding to the movie's black and white photography, and the use of a page organized by a fixed division into regular panels suggesting the constant of the movie screen. *La Dalia Azzura* is hence a revealing paradigm of the new Italian adult comics wherein external cultural materials press against the texture of the text; other telling examples include the employment of found objects in Mattioli, the taste for quotations and self-quotations in Pazienza, and the invasion of the languages of Futurism in Carpinteri.

Also of great significance is Scòzzari's adaptation of Tommaso Landolfi's short story "Il Mar delle Blatte" (The Sea of Roaches) (fig. 3.16). One of the most interesting and elusive Italian writers of the '30s and '40s Landolfi, although active well into the '70s failed to receive critical attention until the 1982 publication of an anthological collection of his writings edited by Italo Calvino. Scòzzari released his take on Landolfi in three installments a few months after the publication of that anthology. Whereas the meeting with Chandler was substantially irreverent, Scòzzari worked side-by-side with Landolfi's writing. After all, Landolfi himself had a great inclination toward destabilizing his own narratives, a prime example being the brilliant exercise in ironic rhetoric that is his short story "Maria Giuseppa" and its unreliable narrator.

Above all, in Landolfi there is a linguistic short circuit at work leading the narrative to question its own mimetic capability: a language that points inward, ultimately becoming the object of the narration and therefore causing a deliberate failure of naturalistic instances that is both liberating and experimental. Under this light the contacts with the poetics of the Italian adult comics are manifold and Scòzzari's successful rendition of a text so difficult to transpose in other media is perhaps one of his greatest achievements. Here, the ironic discourse of the two authors meets halfway and Scòzzari's grotesques work as counterpoints to the deforming effect of Landolfi's language.

In addition to *La Dalia Azzurra*, *Il Mar delle Blatte*, and the *Primo Carnera* saga, while working on *Frigidaire* Scòzzari released a great number of short stories in which the intertextual exchange between genres and news reportage plays a vital role. From 1983 to 1985 he was also responsible for writing the literary reviews column, where he infused his trademark irreverent attitude. In recent years, Scòzzari has entered the literary world with a novel, *Cuore di Edmondo* (1995); a collection of short stories, *Racconti porni* (1996); the autobiographical *Prima pagare poi ricordare* (1997), a lucid, hilarious, and at times touching, recount of the '77 years; the novel

FIG. 3. 16 Scòzzari, Filippo. *Il Mar delle Blatte.*

L'isterico a metano (2001); and the comics manual-cum-childhood autobiography, *Memorie dell' arte bimba* (2008), his last work to date.

STEFANO TAMBURINI AND GAETANO LIBERATORE

In the last two years we exploited the revivals of the '20s, '30s, '40s, '50s, '60s, '70s, and '80s at least thirty times and we launched at least twenty styles for the '90s! I remember all the definitions we had to come up with, from the ridiculous "postmodern" to the current "post-managerial-era nihilism." (Mr. Volare in *Ranxerox*, Tamburini e Liberatore, 1981, 39)

It is necessary to discuss Stefano Tamburini and Gaetano Liberatore together in this section for several reasons, including their artistic partnership in *Cannibale* and *Frigidaire*, and the way in which the two authors ultimately influence and complete one another's work with Liberatore's graphic solutions meshing seamlessly with Tamburini's poetics. Tamburini is one of the key figures in the new adult Italian comics and his work encompasses all the innovations the medium brought about during those years. In a sense, Tamburini is the embodiment of the social and cultural shift that had taken place among the ranks of the proletariat youth toward the end of the '70s: propelling the extreme mobility that saw different tribes (anarchists, *autonomi*, middle-class student activists, suburban proletariat) interact and alternately climb and descend the social ladder throughout the invisible levels of the Italian cities.

Coming from a lower middle-class background, Tamburini grew up in the poor suburbs of Rome and went on to major in philosophy and literature at the University of Rome, where he participated in the student protests that marked those years. By 1975, he had already contributed graphics and stories to the sheets of the Movement (in particular to the journal *Combinazioni*), to supplements to *A/traverso* (the journal founded by Radio Alice's Franco Berardi), and to the independent publishing house Stampa Alternativa. At the height of the political upheaval of '77 Tamburini distanced himself from the politically engaged circles of collectives and founded his own magazine: *Cannibale*. In equal parts *borgataro* (a term that in Roman slang indicates uneducated, underprivileged, suburban dwellers), politically-engaged student, detached anticipator of the post-political generation, and acute spotter of new cultural trends and ideas, Tamburini stands as one of the most paradigmatic intellectual figures of the transition from the late '70s to early '80s.

The two pivotal themes of Tamburini's work are the space and time flattening and the topos of *acceleration*. I already discussed how, by the late '70s, the removal of the great ideological systems had impacted the etiology of artistic creation, with particular immediacy within the field of the visual arts. The eclectic employment of different styles and languages—from Futurism to Dadaism, and from pop art to the popular arts, often within the same framework; the fundamental role played by intertextuality and paratextuality; and the marriage of the abstract and the figurative are all symptoms of a widespread and deeply felt perception of a sudden halt in the dialectical and teleological process of History (that same removal of faith in history that motivated many Marxist critics— Jameson again comes to mind—to dismiss, or at least to suspiciously look at, the development of the arts during those years and to condemn it as a regressive trend). In this regard, the *Ranxerox* saga represents the most exhaustive example of Tamburini's poetics.

The first installment of *Ranxerox*[10] appeared in *Cannibale* in 1978; it was the story of an android built from pieces of photocopy machines by an college student anarchist (a *studelinquente*) who uses his technological Golem to procure drugs, guns, and, in general, to vicariously penetrate the many levels of a multilayered metropolis, gaining access to both the exclusive, aristocratic top tiers inhabited by famous artists and art critics, and to the dangerous low tiers—the haunt of criminals, drug fiends, black marketers, and political dissidents.

Ranxerox's city is a near-future Rome (the late '80s), albeit one radically reinvented. Built on levels (the 38th is the highest Ranxerox ever visits, but the text hints at further heights), Tamburini's Rome not only anticipates the metropolis of Ridley Scott's *Blade Runner*, but it represents a lucid allegory of both the situation of social nomadism the urban youth was experiencing in the late '70s, and more subtly hints at the project of reconfiguring socio-cultural levels the adult comic artists of the time were putting forth with their works. In this perspective, Ranxerox's mobility—his ability to move effortlessly among levels and social strata without belonging to any—clearly reflected the situation of his own readers who inhabited a class-limbo spanning from proletariat to middle class (and it is possible that the reason for the character's immediate success rested to a great degree on the effect of profound identification felt by his readers):

> Rank Xerox was born in '77 on the pages of *Cannibale*. Back then he was a hood with high cheekbones and a short, squashed nose, he had pronounced Asian features, almost a Mongolian. At the time the first contacts between Movement and hoods from the suburbs were taking place: on one side were the students, *studelinquenti*, and the *autonomi*, on the other these hoods, small time criminals, who joined the comrades in the demonstrations and in the squares for reasons of social proximity, sharing the same economic conditions and even coming from the same neighborhoods. They also sided with the Movement in order to find an outlet to their anger, to their inability to bear. Later on the relationship got closer, involving exchange of drugs, etc. Thus in *Ranxerox* a *studelinquente* projects his repressed rage in the mechanical hood he himself built with parts of a photocopy machine stolen from a university building. And he operates it by remote control, remaining safely at home. (Tamburini in *Linus* February 1983, p. 121)

Ranxerox also works as an allegory of the poetics of his creators whose ability to move freely from the low and high levels of the cultural sphere are echoed by the skeleton-key quality of a character who is dealing equally with pushers, hoods, political activists, and multi-millionaire video artists. The metropolis itself embodies one of the main themes of

FIG. 3.17 Tamburini, Stefano and Liberatore, Tanino. *Ranxerox*. The Rome of *Ranxerox* is an accelerated version of the real one: a city where time collapsed on itself. Note the Coliseum (a stratification of metal, cement, and original parts), the new, but already worn by time, *Coliseum Hotel*, and in the background the post-war housing projects. Here artist Liberatore blends late-Renaissance painting and hyper-realism; Ranxerox's hand in the foreground is an explicit Michelangeloesque quote.

Tamburini's work: the compression of time and space. *Ranxerox*'s Rome is in fact a virtual black hole on which, having the course of progress frozen over, space collapsed (fig. 3. 17).

More Las Vegas than Rome in the end, this post-modern metropolis composed of parts of other cities (just like the protagonist is assembled with parts of other machines) expands in the only direction possible: vertically, insisting on its coordinates, feeding on/quoting itself. The result of this time-space compression is twofold and it involves two trademark characteristics of the postmodern: temporal disorientation and spatial decentralization. The former is clearly an effect of the collapse of the category of history; the latter, denouncing the many points of contact of the postmodern ethos with the baroque period, results in a subjective repositioning of spatial coordinates. The dweller of Tamburini's metropolis could very well make his what Italo Calvino's hero claims in *Il conte di Montecristo*: "the center is everywhere I am" (1967).[11]

Intertextuality also plays an important role technically and diegetically. While on this subject, it is worth noting that in the earliest installments of the *Ranxerox* saga Tamburini made extensive use of the photocopy machine by incorporating many found objects and images into its pages. The importance of the photocopy medium in the aesthetics of the Movement was discussed in the previous chapter, but in *Ranxerox* Tamburini manages to tie this technique with the diegetic level of his text by releasing a story about an android composed of parts of a photocopy machine told by way of Xeroxed images. Ranxerox is in fact an intertextual machine that can only experience feelings and express itself by quoting *photocopies* of preexisting thoughts and emotions. Many of Tamburini's stories revolve around this topic.

In the lighthearted *Saturno contro la terra* (1979)—whose title itself quotes another comic, the '40s Italian science-fiction epic by neorealist screenwriter Cesare Zavattini, the enemy civilization of Saturn, bent on conquering the Earth, sends a vanguard of men disguised as earthlings. Unfortunately, all the Saturnians know about our planet is what they have learned from mass media like radio and TV (the story opens with the aliens viewing a 1935 Clark Gable movie). Consequently, the undercover men from Saturn, all of them replicas of Clark Gable and Jean Harlow, can only communicate with earth people by way of quotes from old movies and pop music.

As an inside joke, the language spoken on Saturn itself is a mish-mash of pop culture references—Brian Eno, The Beatles and Skiantos (the *demented rock* band from Bologna tied to the Movement) songs; comic books; and movies. The story ends with the arrival of the Saturnian army, all of them exact replicas of James Cagney in Raul Walsh's *White Heat*. This taste for accumulation of heterogeneous cultural references and the preponderance of *listing* as a discursive device, bringing to mind Rabelais and again the ethos of the baroque has a central role in the *Ranxerox* saga.

In the first episode of *Ranxerox* the titular android enters a bar and is attracted by a jukebox. One panel shows a partial list of the songs: it is

Tamburini's version of the literary topic of the library (those of Borges and Cervantes, but also those of Don Ferrante's in Manzoni's *I promessi Sposi*, and the Prince of Salina's in Lampedusa's *Il gattopardo* come to mind). The difference here is that the written word is substituted by popular music. Inside the jukebox are artists and tracks from diverse musical traditions and geographical areas: late '60s Canterbury art-rocker Robert Wyatt, punk rock New Yorkers The Ramones, Miles Davis, the seminal '77 band from Bologna Gaznevada (at the time they were called Centro d'urlo metropolitano), but also intertextual quotes: the harmonica player Frazz (from a story by Scòzzari) and fictional artists (Johnny Synt in "362 Minutes of Angst"). The chaos of *Ranxerox*'s jukebox clearly reflects that of *Ranxerox*'s metropolis, its loss of historical context.

Cultural quotes and self-references abound throughout the whole saga: TV sets broadcast Massimo Mattioli's *Joe Galaxy*, subway passengers read *Cannibale* and *Frigidaire*, and a celebrated painter visibly resembles Tamburini's real-life idol Mario Schifano, the influential painter and experimental filmmaker who later contributed to *Frigidaire*.

At the end of *Ranxerox*'s first story the android's creator is killed during a police raid and Ranxerox, with his aggressiveness circuits set to maximum as a result of the shoot-out, roams delirious through the streets of Rome. The android, out of control and without a sense of purpose, lives entirely in the context of an equally anarchic and liberating acceleration of emotional states. The liberating feeling that many exponents of the '77 Movement had found in escaping the necessity to "make sense" in *Ranxerox* translates wholly in a decontextualization of feelings, in a flattening of emotional hierarchies.

And it is worth noting once again the way in which the late '70s saw a wide-ranging renewal of interest in the irrationalist legacy of philosophers such as Nietzsche and Heidegger, and how the irrationalist-antipositivistic influence was felt not only in the cultural arena, but remarkably in both the political sphere and in fields such as mathematics and physics. In the works of Tamburini, as well as those of his colleagues at *Cannibale* and *Frigidaire*, the emphasis was on a cooling-off of emotional participation in phenomena of the outside world—a detachment that, as anticipated by Sparagna in the previously quoted editorial of the first issue of *Frigidaire*, allows a wider field of vision and an improved epistemological clarity. Regarding the reconfiguring of emotions in his works, Tamburini once remarked:

FIG. 3.18 Tamburini, Stefano. *Ranxerox*. An early example of photocopy machine use in *Ranxerox*'s first story.

> Rather than the displacement of narrative functions in a script I am interested in emotional displacement . . . in other words I try to preconfigure future emotions. Instead of simply representing hate, or love, or sympathy as we know them today, I try to represent emotions the way they will be in a few years, as filtered by the events that are happening right now. Obviously, in regard to all things, there will be more cynicism . . . but not like in pulp comics where characters are simply cynical, or simply good, or simply adorable. In a story the character's girlfriend could be killed and he might be just slightly annoyed. (www.tiscali.it/tamburini)

Ranxerox's brain is built so that it can produce synthetic emotions. Given three kinds of primary stimuli such as a color, a smell, a vocal timbre, three relays click producing a photocopy of emotion (be it hate, love, or indifference). These mechanical feelings are naturally extremely rudimentary and instable: they change in regards to the same person, if he changes his clothes or his demeanor. (Tamburini, *Ranxerox*, 15)

The first few *Ranxerox* episodes, published in *Cannibale*, were realized by Tamburini with the help of Pazienza, Mattioli, and Scòzzari on pencils, but also with an extended use of found materials and the photocopy machine (fig. 3.18), a technique Tamburini employed in later years, notably in *Snake Agent*. Introduced to the *Cannibale* group by Pazienza, Liberatore's arrival began the Tamburini/Liberatore partnership that lasted until the death of the former in 1986.

Liberatore had previously worked as an illustrator, mostly for record covers for the Italian label RCA, and, with the exception of Pazienza, was the only Cannibale with formal training in fine arts (in fact, the two had met as teenagers at the art school of Pescara). Liberatore's technique can be defined as hyperrealist, although multiple influences in his style are evident and recall diverse artists such as Peter Blake, Carlo Maria Mariani, and Michelangelo. Certainly, the neoclassical quality of Tamburini's art reveals a tight connection to the transversal painters of the '80s but here the magnification of the real becomes a deforming lens, the appropriate tool for Tamburini's penchant for the grotesque.

In this light, Liberatore's art reveals his debts to Flemish painters such as Bosch and Bruegel the elder (also in regards to the use of color), and in general toward early American underground artists of the '60s. Thanks to Liberatore's contribution, the world of *Ranxerox* coalesces into focus and the violence in Tamburini's scripts is documented in a layer of photographic indifference the earlier stories drawn by Tamburini only managed to suggest. In Liberatore's vision the characters and their world appear to be composed of the same matter. Liberatore's careful attention to bodies—their muscles, folds, wrinkles, scars, pox marks—is reflected by the cracks in building walls, pipes and sidewalks; by the cars' dented fenders and by the rust and dust that seem to have consumed *Ranxerox*'s Rome.

The indifference of the narrator and that of his characters translates to an *indifference* (also in the etymological sense of the word) of matter itself. Again, the loss of centrality of the human figure, a process of osmosis with the inanimate matter of its surroundings, evokes the poetics of the baroque. In this undifferentiated world, dynamism and violence

FIG. 3.19 Tamburini, Stefano. *Snake Agent.* An example of Snake Agent's *accelerated* world. This strip can be considered the first, and probably only, instance of "mechanical action painting" in comics. Tamburini often stated that picture manipulation by photocopy machine was a deliberate and difficult process: often more than twenty tries for a single panel were necessary to obtain the desired effect. The fact that Italian artist and designer Bruno Munari (Tamburini was an admirer of his *Useless Machines* sculptures) also dabbled in photocopy art is no coincidence. The balloons in the last panel read: "I'd like a visa for agent Flanagan and myself." "How long do you plan to stay in London, sir?" "Ten, fifteen minutes. Is that too long?"

seem to be the only prerogative to reaffirm the unity of the self. But this aspect of *Ranxerox*'s narrative is kept as an aside in respect to the general poetics of the text. By presenting a future that is simultaneously decrepit and less-than-glamorous, Tamburini and Liberatore, while appropriating anti-positivistic and anti-teleological stances of their time, are far from presenting a dystopian rhetoric (a concern rather ascribable to the genre of science fiction). Instead *Ranxerox*'s discourse revolves entirely around a conspicuous ideological detachment on the author's part so that the

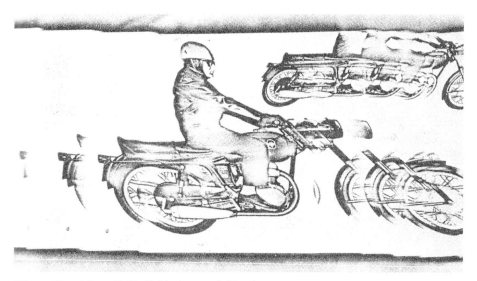

FIG. 3.20   Munari, Bruno. *Untitled "original xerography"* (1977).

world represented, besides the evident enjoyment in the portrayal of the chaos that constitutes it, resists allegorical interpretations.

Parallel to his work on *Ranxerox*, Tamburini worked on *Snake Agent*, a comic strip wherein the intertextual play is more manifest, albeit with deeper implications. To realize *Snake Agent*, Tamburini used a preexisting American strip from the '40s: reproducing and deforming it through the photocopy machine and rewriting its dialogue balloons and captions (fig. 3.19), a process that refers to and develops artist Bruno Munari's late '70s experiments with the medium (fig. 3.20).

Narrative acceleration dominates this work: not only do the characters move spatially from continent to continent in a few seconds (an ironic, self-referential meditation on the elliptical nature of comic book narration), but their moods shift from love to hate, and from bravado to fear in the space of a single panel. A "cannibal" comic in the true sense of the word, feeding as it does on another comic strip, *Snake Agent* is probably the most "postmodern" of all the creations of the *Frigidaire* group as it favors manipulation of preexisting materials over the superstition of original creation, performance over finite work, and the grotesque over the romantic.

Although comparisons to Roy Lichtenstein's works come to mind—the employment of an *objet trouvè* from the area of popular culture—*Snake*

FIG. 3.21 Tamburini, Stefano. Untitled illustration for *Frigidaire*.

Agent is rooted in pastiche rather than parody, developing its own discourse much along the lines of Scòzzari's adaptation of Chandler's *Blue Dahlia*. Where pop art, almost with an alchemic agenda, employed comics to realize works of "art" destined for art galleries and museums, Tamburini's *Snake Agent* embraces its aesthetic but brings it full circle it by again producing comics. Additionally, the employment of the photocopy machine—a medium that, unlike photography, is meant to specifically reproduce texts (albeit deforming them) rather than the empirical world—works as a declaration of intent for the whole phenomenon of the new adult comics: it insists on the centrality of the cultural data and the necessity of manipulation.

As noted in the last chapter, much of Tamburini's work deals with surfaces. On the narrative level, dealing with surfaces means stripping one's characters of psychological depth (Ranxerox, the android whose processors allow him only basic and arbitrary emotional reactions, is a plain example of this stance) and deflecting the suspicion of a conspicuously present ideological component. On the graphic level, Tamburini translates his attention to surfaces through the use of the photocopy machine, a device that produces only highly contrasted versions of the original materials. Later in his career he employed monochromatic cut-outs to create flattened-out figures (fig. 3.21), insisting once again on the primacy of composition in the creative process.

Along with his narrative work, Tamburini was also responsible for the design of *Frigidaire*, infusing the magazine with a dry and "fast" look highly indebted to the suprematist painters. In the last years of his career he ventured into the field of fashion and began work on a clothing line, *Scrooge*, for a Milanese company, which employed his trademark cut-outs. He also tried his hand at commercial design for the pharmaceutical company Pfizer.

Among the authors of the Italian new adult comics, Tamburini stands as one of the most aesthetically complex and certainly the one whose work boasted the greatest wealth of referents—from popular culture and music to that of the high arts. In his works the comic books of the '40s and '50s, science fiction B-movies, the conceptual art of Piero Manzoni, the rigor of Piet Mondrian, both Russian and Italian Futurism, and the admiration for painter and filmmaker Mario Schifano, artist/designer Bruno Munari, and neoavantgardist visual poet Adriano Spatola all somehow coexist. To this day, the *Ranxerox* stories Tamburini and Liberatore created are among the few examples of the Italian adult comics that have found an audience abroad, having been published in France, Spain, Germany, Holland, the United States, Greece, Finland, and Japan.

MASSIMO MATTIOLI

Multiple coding—where two or more different and antithetical reading possibilities within a single text—coexist—sits at the heart of the great majority of the works of new adult comics artists. For example,

FIG. 3.22 Mattioli, Massimo. *Squeak the Mouse*. The punch line of the first *Squeak the Mouse* installment rests entirely in a sudden shift from innocent cartoon slapstick to gory violence. The last two panels are a nod to black and white American cartoons of the '30s.

in Scòzzari's *Dalia Azzurra* the two layers are constituted by Chandler's romantic mode and the grotesque of its comic book adaptation. In *Snake Agent*, the layering articulates along the level of the story, its visual discourse, and the shadow of its paratext—the original American strip employed and manipulated by Tamburini.

Among the authors discussed in this book, Mattioli is the one who most consistently made multiple coding the center of his aesthetics. One of the original contributors to *Cannibale*, Mattioli had already published in France in the magazine *Pif*, and in Italy—first in the venerable young adults' Catholic comic magazine, *Il Vittorioso*, in the newspaper, *Paese Sera*, then in *Il Giornalino*. For the latter, a magazine aimed at children and published by the Vatican's own publishing house, Edizioni Paoline, Mattioli had a steady job drawing the adventures of a pink rabbit called Pinky.

When Mattioli began creating stories for *Cannibale*'s adult audience, he imported his child-oriented drawing style and storytelling, merging them with the adult content of the magazine. The end result, at least for his earliest work in the adult comics canon, recalls the aesthetic of the American underground comics, particularly that of Robert Crumb. Mattioli's work for *Cannibale* is populated by cute, cartoon-like characters (derivatives of the Tex Avery, Fleischer Studios, and Warner Brothers iconographies) maliciously dropped into adult situations wherein slapstick comedy often culminates in realistic physical violence or overtly sexual situations (fig. 3.22).

This opposition between form and content, the true power of the adult comics, worked primarily because of the resulting strong effect of displacement. In this case, the expectations suggested by the puppet-like renderings of the characters were challenged by the adult content of the stories. In his later contributions to *Frigidaire*, Mattioli further complicated the simple mechanics of this approach. In particular, the *Joe Galaxy e le perfide lucertole di Callisto IV* saga, published in monthly installments from 1980 to 1981, expanded this schizophrenic strategy to the level of discourse. First, the use of color—bright, solid yellows, reds, and blues in line with the graphic project of the magazine—quoted Mondrian's compositions, with the painter's squares translated into the narrative panels of the comic book form. As a result, *Joe Galaxy*'s pages read two ways: as a series of narrative units represented by the panels and as a synchronic painterly whole.

Secondly, Mattioli intertwined his trademark pen and ink cartoonish style with a pictorial one, arbitrarily inserting panels drawn with brush and acrylics or created from external, found objects such as photos, film stills, and magazine ads. This eclectic approach, noted in the works of Pazienza, reveals Mattioli's strong debt to early pop art, especially British artists belonging to the Independent Group such as Eduardo Paolozzi and Richard Hamilton.

Given Mattioli's medium, his work plays a double twist on early pop art. While painters like Hamilton were integrating popular imagery into high-art, Mattioli employed pop images filtered through pop art (by the '80s a canonized moment of modern high-art) and placed them again in

FIG. 3.23 Mattioli, Massimo. *Joe Galaxy e le perfide lucertole di Callisto IV.*

a popular media context: the comic book form. One could say that the pop-art circle closes only in the postmodern '80s, with the return of its materials to the point of origin. Lastly, in *Joe Galaxy*, Mattioli plays with the organization of the page: at times self-consciously adopting a rigorous grid division à la Hergé, and at others intentionally disrupting it with the intrusion of discordant elements.

In the opening episode of the saga, for example, the first page is divided into six panels of equal dimensions, while the following page is divided horizontally in two sections—the first section, in a blue monochrome recalling the screen of a TV monitor, is occupied by a flashback to the events narrated in the first page (fig. 3.23). The following page is again divided in two, this time vertically. The first column is composed of three panels of equal dimensions and the second hosts a fictional commercial break advertising space-age sex toys with a collage of found materials. The whole third installment of *Joe Galaxy* is presented as a double LP, each page representing one side of the record, and each panel a song (coherently, Mattioli also indicates the "playing time" of each panel). In opposition, the following episode is entirely organized by way of a strict grid of same-size panels.

This experimentally playful approach to the internal structure of the page, and consequently to the graphic and narrative rhythm of the text, is by no means a novelty in the context of comics. In Italy, one of the first authors to test and expand the possibilities of organization of the comic book page was Guido Crepax. As early as the '60s, with his *Valentina*, Crepax had experimented with a cinematic montage of the comic book narration playing with the variable dimension of his panels to suggest camera movements and duration of "shots." Then in the '70s the French authors of *Metal Hurlant* made the reconfiguration of the structure of the comic book page one of the central concerns of their aesthetics. But with Mattioli, the main difference is that his structural idiosyncrasies appear to be somehow independent from diegetic concerns.

In other words, while with the authors of the *fumetto d'autore* of the '60s the experimentation with structures was motivated by a need to expand the narrative horizons of the comic book form, and with the French authors of the '70s the structures themselves became the center of their work (often to the detriment of narrative coherence), with Mattioli the comic book text reveals a deliberate split—it is equally aesthetic object and narrative machine. The proof is that Mattioli's pages, especially in his work during the '80s, conspicuously offer both a synchronic (aesthetic) reading and a diachronic (narrative) one.

LE BOCCHE DA FUOCO PUNTARONO SUL GRUPPO DI ANGELI E SPARARONO ALL'IMPAZZATA.

FIG. 3.24 Mattioli, Massimo. *Guerra*. Eclecticism is one of the key features of Mattioli's work in the '80s. For this story, Mattioli adopted a painterly style by momentarily abandoning pen and ink for brush and oil.

Mattioli continued contributing to *Frigidaire* until the mid-'80s with a series of shorter, markedly eclectic works, each rich in references to both the popular and high arts. In stories such as *Ingordo, Frisk the Frog, Sea of Hate*, and *Magma* quotes from painters Richard Hamilton and Andy Warhol appear, along with references to the optical and kinetic art of Bridger Riley, the Tex Avery cartoons, '50s American EC horror comics, and directors David Cronenberg and Lucio Fulci. Throughout this period of his career Mattioli intensified the use of heterogeneous graphic styles. As a result his *Frigidaire* stories feature pen-and-ink caricatural puppet renditions, brush-and-oil painterly panels, photographic images, and found materials (fig. 3.24).

Of all the creators of the new adult comics, Mattioli perhaps most closely embodies Achille Bonito Oliva's notion that "to be an artist now it means to have everything in front of oneself as in a kind of spatial synchronicity" (Oliva, 1981, 6). In the late '80s, Mattioli and Pazienza migrated to the pages of *Comic Art* while simultaneously publishing in France in the satirical magazine *L'Écho des savanes*. His later output, though more conventionally narrative, still retains much of the inventiveness of his early efforts. Along with Tamburini, Mattioli was one of a handful of Italian new adult comic book artists published extensively abroad. Almost the entirety of Mattioli's work was published in France, and a few of his stories have been published in book form in the United States.

THE VALVOLINE GROUP

Aside from the artists associated with *Frigidaire*, the only other group of adult comic creators active in the '80s were tied to the magazines *Linus* and *Alter*. The *Valvoline* group, whose members included Lorenzo Mattotti, Igort (Igor Tuveri), Daniele Brolli, Marcello Jori, Jerry Kramsky, and for a brief period the American cartoonist Charles Burns, formed in Bologna in January 1983. In the same year, the group's works appeared throughout seven consecutive issues of *Alter* in a section that took up most of the pages of the magazine.

Also in 1983, the group founded *Zio Feininger* (a reference to Lyonel Feininger, painter, pioneer of comics, and author of *The Kin-der-Kids*), a "school of comics" that counted Andrea Pazienza and Filippo Scòzzari among its professors. The school helped to produce the next generation of Italian comic artists, a generation unfortunately penalized by the crisis that hit in the mid-'80s. Among the authors who learned or honed their skills at *Zio Feininger* were Giuseppe Palumbo (a regular in *Frigidaire* in the late '80s and early '90s), Gabriella Giandelli, and Francesca Ghermandi, the latter widely published in the United States and among the best of the contemporary Italian comic artists. Valvoline later launched its own magazine, *Dolce Vita* (1987–1989), which soon folded because of low sales.

The group represented a moderate line compared to the aesthetics of the *Frigidaire* artists. In fact, having found a home first in the pages of *Linus* and later at *Alter*, they sought a middle ground between the old auteurs and the new adult comics. Furthermore, while the *Frigidaire* artists found their materials in highly diverse fields, the *Valvoline* group focused on the world of painting (privileging the historical avant-gardes and turn-of-the-century European art), typically with a lyrical leaning that became particularly evident in the works of Mattotti.

Certainly, the import of the references, intentionally distinct within the works of *Frigidaire* artists such as Mattioli or Tamburini, is sensibly fuzzier in the output of the *Valvoline* group. Thus, in these comics, the textual strategy points aesthetically towards the sum of the parts rather

FIG. 3.25 Carpinteri and Jori. *Rumble Mumble*. In this story about earthquakes drawn by Carpinteri and colored by fellow *Valvoline* artist Jori, the triangular shape is the main geometrical building block in this panel. Note the expressionistic use of perspective and the Futurist quotes (particularly Balla and Depero): the motif on the lampshade, the flowers on the right, and especially the folds of the curtains held by the protagonist. Also note how the panel's careful composition is crossed by a zigzag line indicating the left-to-right reading order. Starting from the top left corner, the line is formed by the pots jumping on the stove, the clock falling off the wall, the lamp, the right forearm of the protagonist, his shoulders, the left arm—culminating in the triangular mass of the curtains. A visual shock wave, this is one of the best examples of Carpinteri's panel composition. Published in the pages of *Frigidaire*, the story *Rumble Mumble* was also complemented by an audio track by the band Stupid Set (featuring members of Gaznevada and Confusional Quartet), *Hear the Rumble*, which was meant to be played as the story is read (the album was sold separately). A year later, the story received a second aural homage: the song *Kaspar's Spring* (Kaspar is the name of the protagonist of *Rumble Mumble*). The composition appeared on the eponymous second album by the Bolognese band Central Unit, whose cover art was by Carpinteri.

than to the destabilizing effect of the quote. In this regard, Carpinteri's work represents an anomaly in the context of the *Valvoline* aesthetics.

Before joining Valvoline, Giorgio Carpinteri was the youngest artist in the *Frigidaire* group. Like Scòzzari, his work debuted in *Il Mago* and he later contributed to such short-lived publications as *Il Pinguino* and *Nemo*. Graphically speaking, the main influence on Carpinteri's style can be traced to the Italian futurists and in particular the rigid geometrical and chromatic solutions of painter and designer Fortunato Depero (fig. 3.25). In this self-conscious quoting strategy Carpinteri is much closer in spirit to the *Frigidaire* group, and he is easily "the least lyrical and the most constructivist and formalist among the *Valvoline* authors" (Barbieri, 12, 1990).

Carpinteri's first contribution to *Frigidaire*, "Incrocio magico," which appeared in 1981, is particularly indicative of his early style. The story is

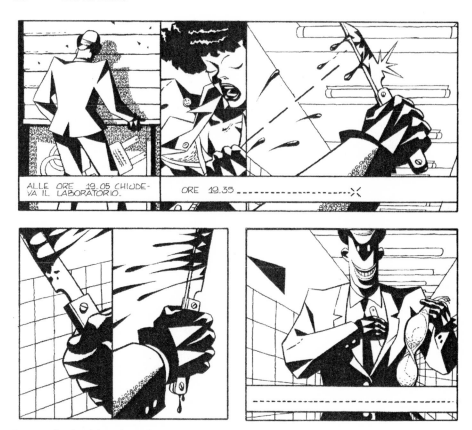

FIG. 3.26 Carpinteri. *Incrocio magico.*

told by way of sharp contrasts of black and whites and the few half-tone effects are rendered by the repetition of the word "ombra" (shadow). The figures are simplified and rendered through geometrical shapes, mostly triangular volumes carefully organized within the panels (fig. 3.26). Once again (as mentioned regarding the works of Tamburini and Mattioli), whenever referring to modernist aesthetics, the *Frigidaire* artists specifically privilege rational constructivism over abstract expressionism; accordingly, in Carpinteri we also find echoes of Mondrian and Moholy Nagy, in addition to the obvious references to Depero and the Russian Futurists. Indeed, the centrality of the constant interplay of geometrical shapes in Carpinteri's work recalls the poetics of the surface found in Tamburini's graphic output. In fact, in 1982 the two artists collaborated on the story "Notti bianche."

FIG. 3.27 Carpinteri. *Rumble Mumble.* These panels present a postmodern microcosm of twentieth-century iconographies: De Chirico's architectural landscapes, German expressionism, Futurist geometrical constructivism, '40s poster art, and the "new wave" '80s look of the figure to the extreme right of the panel. In respect to the other Valvoline artists, Carpinteri favors accumulation over assimilation.

"Incrocio magico" is also rife with quotes that range from the low- to the highbrow. The protagonist of the story is a metaphysical serial killer who dresses like his favorite comic book character, Il signor Bonaventura. The choice of Sergio Tofano's Bonaventura is particularly meaningful because it was an Italian children's favorite throughout the early twentieth century, and Tofano's strip was one of the very few comics of the period to employ Futurist solutions in comics, therefore suggesting the possibility of a double reading. Certainly, besides the function of grotesque attained by the debasement of a beloved children's comic book character to the role of serial killer (much in tune with Mattioli's poetics), Carpinteri meant the reference to Tofano as homage to an illustrious pioneer of cultural transversalism. In "Incrocio magico" Carpinteri even managed a self-referential aside—in a story so graphically dominated by geometrical shapes the protagonist is a collector of polyhedrons that he hangs daily on top of his bathtub to water like houseplants.

Diegetically, Carpinteri's violent and heavily surreal stories reveal the author's fascination with French authors such as Eugene Ionesco, Boris Vian, and Raymond Queneau. In 1982, Carpinteri abandoned black and white in favor of color and the pictorial references broadened to include the metaphysical paintings of De Chirico (fig 3.27). His first published color story, again in the pages of *Frigidaire*, was a collaboration with soon-to-be *Valvoline* colleague Marcello Jori. In 1983, with the foundation of the *Valvoline* group Carpinteri published mostly in the pages of *Alter* and by the late '80s abandoned comics altogether in order to concentrate on his work on advertising campaigns and as a set designer for RAI, the Italian national TV.

While the other Valvoline authors were primarily comics artists who incorporated pictorial languages into their works, Marcello Jori was an exception to the rule—he was primarily a painter who found himself working in comics. Anticipating to some degree the research of the *Frigidaire* artists, Jori, already an affirmed painter, began publishing his comic strip *Minus* in the pages of *Linus* as early as 1977. His initial output in the comic book field recalls the work of painter Paul Klee in its chromatic solutions and its bittersweet primitivism, while the light-hearted cruelty of his punch lines calls to mind the visual work of surrealist Roland Topor.

In 1980 Jori joined the *Nuovi Nuovi*, which, under the aegis of neo-avant-garde theorist Renato Barilli, was one of the most important groups of painters of the decade. The *Nuovi Nuovi*, which included painters such as Giuseppe Maraniello, Vittorio Messina, Luigi Ontani, and Felice Levini, was, if it was possible, an even less homogeneous group than that of the *trans-avant-garde*. Its artists referred both to conceptual and behavioral art, frequently employing other media such as music and literature, and often experimenting in the field of video art. Though possessing a more marked ironic vein, the *Nuovi Nuovi* shared with the painters of the *Trans-avant-garde* a drive toward the figurative that set them apart from painters of previous decades.

In 1982, Jori participated in the prestigious *Biennale di Venezia* (he contributed again in 1993) and began exhibiting in many important international galleries and museums, among them the Studio Marconi in Milan, the Hayward Gallery of London, and the Holly Solomon in New York. When Jori joined the Valvoline group in 1983, he abandoned both the use of color and the stylized rendition of his early cartoon work to concentrate on an hyperrealist style, which he obtained through the use of photographs (developing, just like Tamburini and Mattioli, a personal poetics of the *objet trouvè*) and a strict palette of white and greys (fig. 3.28):

> At some point I noticed that the group (Valvoline) was becoming, also style-wise, very compact. And in that compactness I perceived the weakness of the group itself, the danger of being too immediately recognizable. Therefore I decided to be the most different element in the group,

FIG. 3.28   Jori, Marcello. *Cuore di soldato, orologio del mondo.*

the one whose works would stand the passing of time. (. . .) So I asked myself what mode is the hardest to adopt when you want to make avant-garde, when you want to make experimental work? Realism. I went in the opposite direction of the group. I decided to literally brutalize the group and I chose to be a realist to the end. I therefore started from photography. (Jori in Barbieri 1990, 87)

Jori abandoned comics in the mid '80s but returned to the medium from 1992 to 1998 with a series of works commissioned exclusively for the Japanese publishing house Kodansha. And most recently, he has written prose fiction. Jori's first novel, *Nonna Picassa*, was published in 2000 by the prestigious publishing house, Mondadori. A testimony of the strong interrelation between the new adult comics and contemporary painting during the early '80s, Jori's work stands as one of the most exemplary and successful instances of transgression of the arbitrary divides between high- and lowbrow art and, most significantly, between high- and lowbrow media.

Daniele Brolli also played an important role, and, like Carpinteri, participated in both the *Valvoline* and *Frigidaire* groups. However, while Carpinteri was mostly a cartoonist, Brolli primarily contributed scripts and articles (though he was also an artist and occasionally produced comics as well). For *Frigidaire*, Brolli essentially worked as a translator for the foreign articles and literature hosted by the magazine, and it was he who signed translations of the unpublished short works of such authors as J.G. Ballard and Chester Himes. In reality, many of Brolli's translations were actually creative works commissioned by various publishers and penned by the translator himself.

Brolli revealed the scam only recently with the publication of a collection of his best forgeries: *Segreta identità* (1996).[12] Thus, Brolli and the *Frigidaire* staff followed in the tradition of the *fakes* that was at the heart of the philosophy of counter-information of the '77 Movement and that was later institutionalized by the weekly *Il Male*. In Brolli's work it is the concept of signature and authenticity that is specifically challenged: writing in a particular author's voice means, above all, to participate and have one's readers participate in a set of cultural choices.

The horizon of culture is therefore ultimately that of culture itself: a postmodern paradigm that has indeed outlived the high-postmodern decade of the '80s—one need only consider the relevance today of slippery issues such as those regarding authorship and the legitimacy of copyright.

Brolli is also responsible for baptizing the Italian *Cannibali* writers of the '90s. In 1996, he edited and wrote the introduction for the first anthology of these young authors, *Gioventù Cannibale*; the name was clearly meant as a tribute to Tamburini's magazine, *Cannibale*, and the influence it exerted on many of the anthologized authors. Certainly the import of the debt to the *Frigidaire* group is notable especially in the early efforts of writers such as Aldo Nove, Niccolò Ammaniti, Andrea G. Pinketts, and Daniele Luttazzi.

However, while most of the critics stressed the affiliation with the adult comics because of the violence contained in these narratives (*splatter literature* was an alternative label used to indicate the works of the *Cannibali*), they failed to register a deeper connection. On one hand, this affinity of poetics was rooted in the predilection for a language that was not only *fast*, but also permeable, open as it was to urban slang and the elliptic quality of the rhetoric of mass media; on the other hand was a common appetite for cross-cultural references ranging from game shows to Shakespeare, from Stephen King to Giacomo Leopardi. So, with Brolli the circle seemed to close, from the debut of Tamburini's *Cannibale* in 1977 to the translation of the same materials in a high cultural area with the Cannibali writers (although, truth be told, these latter never achieved the impact of their comic-making namesakes).

Lorenzo Mattotti is the most renowned Valvoline and has enjoyed the greatest degree of success abroad, particularly in comics-friendly countries like France and the United States where his stories appeared in the

FIG. 3.29 Mattotti, Lorenzo. *Il Signor Spartaco.*

'80s in Art Spiegelman's *RAW*. In addition to contributing to magazines such as *Linus* and *Alter* since the late '70s, his works are currently issued by the venerable literary publishing house Einaudi. And outside comics Mattotti worked in cinema, notably designing the titles connecting the three episodes of *Eros*, the Antonioni, Soderbergh, and Won Kar-Wai film. His recent contribution to the animated episode-movie, *Peur(s) du Noir* (2007), where he reunited with fellow Valvoline Charles Burns, received enthusiastic reviews in the United States. Mattotti is the *most painterly* of the Valvoline artists and in fact, at the heart of all his mature work is the desire to mediate between the mediums of painting and comics:

> It is important to see if it is possible to expand the field of comics. At least to try before claiming that it is impossible. Sometimes I found myself on dead end streets, leaning too far toward conceptuality or the world of painting. In *Fires* (1985) I think one can sense a strong tension between painting, narrative, and the private sphere. The important thing is to find an equilibrium which will allow everything to be preserved and nothing to be destroyed. Sometimes it happened that when there were certain feelings I wanted to express, images of painters I loved and that spoke my some language would come to the forefront. It was therefore natural to accept their suggestions, to follow their lessons. Certainly I can at times also be detached, aware of the sources of my inspiration. But it is always imperative for me to feel that I completely appropriated those sources in order to employ them. (Mattotti in Barbieri 1990, 109)

Mattotti's early works, in the pages of *Linus*, were more conventional in style. Often scripted by Jerry Kramsky (also part of the Valvoline group) and betraying the influence of the Argentinian comic authors Muñoz and Sampayo, these early efforts centered on life in the suburbs and hinterlands of Italy. These short stories, because of their low-key realism and understated climaxes, recalled the up-and-coming American minimalist writers of the '80s rather than the Italian neorealist tradition.

The turning point for Mattotti came in 1982 with the publication of the long story "Il signor Spartaco" in *Alter*. Mattotti used color consistently for the first time here, employing mostly oil crayons and pictorial references that spanned the Futurists to Matisse (fig. 3.29). With his subsequent work, "Fuochi," also for *Alter*, Mattotti reached full maturity and abandoned the black contour lines typical of comics, instead utilizing a full painterly style based on contrapositions of volumes and chiaroscuros.

Among his later works, his full-length adaptation of Stevenson's *The Strange Case of Dr. Jekyll and Mr. Hyde* was particularly noteworthy. Here, along the usual references, Mattotti turned to German expressionism and the works of Otto Dix. A minimalist storyteller with a maximalist visual style and at times uneven in his writing—but always graphically innovative, Mattotti stands with the most important Italian comic artists of recent decades.

Finally, of the many authors who contributed to *Valvoline*, the most prolific at this time is Igort (Igor Tuveri), a comic book artist whose work is chiefly notable for his editorial efforts in connection with the publishing house Coconino. The most important comic book publishing house in Italy today, Coconino released books by leading foreign adult comic artists such as the Hernandez Brothers and Charles Burns (U.S.), Jiro Taniguchi (Japan), and Baru (France), along with many new and established Italian artists including himself, Gipi, Andrea Bruno, and Lorenzo Mattotti.

Overall, when compared to those of *Frigidaire*, the individual Valvoline authors have enjoyed longer artistic careers, as many are still active and successfully weathered the transformation of the comic book form in the last decade. Indeed, if by definition the destiny of any avant-garde movement is to make a decisive break with traditional aesthetics and eventually disintegrate once its drive is exhausted, the Valvoline authors owe their artistic longevity to their moderate approach and less antagonistic relationship with their sources: establishing tight connections with the auteur comics tradition while imparting their own personal brand of formal innovations.

Conclusions

As the '80s drew to a close, so did the Italian adult comics movement. This change was paralleled throughout the industry, particularly in France, but to a lesser degree in the American market. In addition to the premature departure of two of its leading figures, Tamburini and Pazienza, one contributing factor to the Italian adult comics' decline was the dramatic increase in the cost of printing paper—which forced many publications out of the market.[1]

But on a deeper level, behind the crisis of the adult comics were the profound changes the generation of '77, representing the readership of publications such as *Cannibale*, *Il Male*, and *Frigidaire*, experienced throughout the '80s. The illusion of a second economic boom during the socialist government of Prime Minister Bettino Craxi and the harsh police repression—beginning after the assassination of Aldo Moro and continuing after the bombing of the Bologna train station—effectively destroyed what little remained of the Movement. This then dissolved the elusive new social subject that, for almost a decade, constituted a novel urban hybrid between proletariat and middle class and thus served as the ideal audience for the adult comics.

A uniform urban middle class composed mostly of shopkeepers and independent entrepreneurs quick to seek the advantages of what was thought to be a new economic miracle took its place.[2] It should be noted that the Movement was primarily composed of students and that by the '80s most of them had slipped back into the ranks of society in an awkward, but inevitable, repetition of the post-'68 situation. At the same time, the generation that should have provided a fresh audience for the adult comics' readership instead regarded this medium as an anachronism, having been reared on much "faster" media, television in particular.

Further, the '80s was also the decade in which future Prime Minister Silvio Berlusconi's financial empire came to the forefront in the media arena, thanks in part to his friendships in the ranks of the Socialist Party. The explosion of small, privately owned radio and TV stations that emerged in the mid-'70s lasted only a short time. In 1978 there were more than 500 private TV stations in Italy—a stunning *per capita* if compared with the 900 stations operating at the same time in the United States.[3] But by the early '80s, only a handful of local TV stations remained, the majority having been bought out or forced out of business by Berlusconi's Fininvest monopoly which, along with his three national channels (Italia 1, Rete 4 and Canale 5) would from that point forward represent the only competitor to RAI, the state-owned national TV channels.

Berlusconi's channels successfully imposed a general trivialization of taste on the Italian audiences through the persistent broadcasting of Reagan-era Hollywood movies, American TV series, and soaps, and the non-stop flow of commercials emphasizing images of available luxury—a far cry from the rhetoric of "moderate wealth for everyone" sponsored by the Christian Democrats since the '50s. For better or worse, this media-driven rhetoric shaped the collective imagination of a generation.

The impact of this TV-dominated decade is still felt in Italy today where political campaigns are fought not only by broadcast debates and speeches, but in a much subtler way—by programming that superimposes the fictional world of TV series, talk shows, and game shows over the political programs and electoral promises of the candidates. And so it was in, and because of, this climate of oppressive mass-media domination that comics literacy (one has to know how to read comics in order to understand and decipher their structures and codes, just as one learns how to read poetry or fiction) dramatically decreased into a resulting crisis—not only with adult comics, but with those aimed at younger readers as well.

By the end of the '80s, the three most important adult comic magazines in France (*Metal Hurlant*, *Fluide Glacial*, and *A suivre*) folded in rapid succession. Similarly, in Italy venerable comics magazines such as *Alter*, *Il Mago*, and *Eureka* also closed their doors within the decade, and the last of the adult comic pillars, *Linus*, was reduced to a monthly collection of syndicated American comic strips. Magazines of great quality, such as *La Dolce Vita*, lasted only a few issues as did a handful of doomed attempts to rehash the old adventure stories of the *auteur* comics with magazines such as *Orient Express* (whose greatest merit was that of introducing the works of Magnus to a new generation of readers of auteur comics) and *Corto Maltese* (in whose pages appeared a misplaced and unconvincing Pazienza).

Interestingly, the top-selling Italian comic book series in the late '80s and '90s was Tiziano Sclavi's *Dylan Dog*, a pulp horror publication aimed at young adults. *Dylan Dog* narratives were imbedded with intertextual references (pulp and B-movies specifically), and it configured itself as a sort of soft late-post-modern meta-narrative. By the early '90s, what remained of the Italian market was overrun by Japanese manga and American superhero comics. Attempts at resuscitating the auteur magazine comics, such as *Fuego* and *Cyborg* (edited by Daniele Brolli), were short-lived.

Presently, however, a gradual, consistent, renewed interest in adult comics in Italy is occurring, as publishers like Coconino Press and young artists such as Gipi and Ghermandi clearly demonstrate. The difference is that, in the new millennium, adult comics have disappeared from newsstands only to resurface in proper bookstores. In the '70s, comics in France and Italy were occasionally repackaged in book form, but this is the first time comics have bypassed monthly serialization and are instead being produced in book form and targeted specifically to bookstores rather than newsstands.

Certainly, this trend owes much to the so-called "graphic novel," a format that soared in popularity in the United States in the '80s, and the success of which was due in part to the popularity of stores dedicated to comics—a fixture in America since the late '60s. Paralleling the Italian experience of new adult comics and magazines such as *Frigidaire*, the innovative American publication *RAW* (edited by Art Spiegelman, author of the successful epic *Maus*) had anticipated the trend of the comic book as book *tout court*. Distributed exclusively in bookstores, adorned with eye-catching post-modern graphics, and sold at a purposely expensive price meant to impart prestige, *Raw* presented itself as a cross between art-book and literary product. This trend continues to this day in the United States, with distinguished publications such as *Blab* and *Mome*, and is reflected by the present-day Italian publishing industry.

It is certain though, that the disappearance from the newsstands deprived the Italian adult comics of that chance for interplay with actuality, that journalistic component that characterized some of its most vital examples, from *Il Male* to *Frigidaire*. Ever closer to the fiction section of the bookstores that carry them, present-day adult comics are increasingly becoming *literary objects* closely identified with a well-defined cultural canon, a notion the comic artists of the '70s and '80s might not have entertained, but one that might very well constitute their ticket to a long life in the decades to come.

As a final note, I'd like to refer to a single-panel cartoon by Andrea Pazienza, published posthumously in 1988. In the panel, a young student protester is shown exiting a time machine after a trip to the mid-'80s. As he steps out, back into 1978, he bemoans: "Guys, it's a disaster! The rising sun of the Socialist Party is shining, Cossiga [conservative minister of internal affairs during the harsh repression following Moro's kidnapping and sworn enemy of the Movement] is president! We've lost everything!" Besides the immediate humor of the situation, resting on the complete and all-too-real defeat of a generation, Pazienza's cartoon hits a more subtle target: the flash-like changes that impacted the generation of '77 during the first half of the '80s.

This sense of displacement, which overnight turned the '77 students and activists into a generation of Rip Van Winkles—confused time-travelers—corresponds to the perception of a sudden end of both alternative political strategies and of a specific cultural cycle. If the new adult comics can be employed as a clue of sorts, tightly interconnected as they were to other experiences in the cultural arena, then the eclipse of the medium corresponding to the late '80s and most of the '90s is certainly proof of this abrupt turn—of the existence of a cultural black hole rooted in the Berlusconi-dominated late '80s and '90s and whose pull is in some measure still felt today.

This is not to say the new adult comics did not succeed in leaving a legacy. As previously noted, it was during those very '90s that witnessed a virtual disappearance of the medium that the influence of the *Cannibale*, *Frigidaire*, and *Valvoline* artists was felt once again, this time in the field of literature. Authors like Scarpa, Nove, Ammaniti, and many other young writers who began their artistic career in that decade clearly developed in the '80s under the influence of the works of Pazienza, Scòzzari, and Tamburini.

Certainly, the new adult comics provided an escape from the still somewhat claustrophobic Italian cultural environment. Their major accomplishments remain: the defense of multiculturalism and plurilinguism, the criticism of the old official left with its parochialism, and the constant trespassing of the divide between lowbrow and highbrow art. Also, at a twenty-year distance, they give back a strikingly articulate image of a particularly troubled, but culturally lively time in the life of the Italian Republic—a period whose investigation and rediscovery calls for the study of these comic artists and their work as its starting point.

Notes

CHAPTER ONE

1. The first comic book hosting original material, *New Fun*, appeared in the United States in 1935.

2. *Giallo* (yellow) is the name Italians gave to the *whodunit* genre. Differing theories explain the choice of the color yellow to tag detective stories. The one commonly accepted refers to the popularity of a series of whodunit novels published by Mondadori. Appearing in 1929, censored by the Fascist regime, and resurfacing in the immediate post-war years, all volumes in the series sported a trademark yellow cover. From the '70s forward, the term *giallo* is used—mostly abroad and especially in English-speaking countries—in reference to a special brand of Italian murder mystery movies.

3. In 1960, under pressure of the Christian Democratic Party and on charges of obscenity, Fellini's *La Dolce Vita* risked being seized and severely edited. Fellini jokingly commented on the episode with the short *Le Tentazioni del Dottor Antonio* in 1962.

4. A great admirer of Bava's work, Fellini cast Barbara Steele in his *Eight and a Half*, as the alluring British girlfriend of Guido's old friend, Mezzabotta. Fellini later quoted Bava again in his *Toby Dammit* by borrowing the image of the evil ball-bearing ghost girl from *Operazione Paura*.

5. EC Comics (of *Tales from the Crypt* and *Mad* fame) had a similar function in the United States in the mid-'50s, as its horror titles (with all the gore but none of the sex of their Italian successors) provoked a violent anti-comics crusade that changed the perception of the medium and opened the doors for the rise of underground comics a decade later.

6. Pratt authored two adaptations from Stevenson's works: *Treasure Island* in 1964 and *Kidnapped* the following year.

7. In 1948, Italy began receiving full economic aid from the United States as part of the Marshall Plan. On March 20, 1948, a few weeks before the elections, George Marshall publicly declared that in the case of a Communist victory all financial help to Italy would have been suspended.

8. On March 28, 1948, Pope Pio XII warned Christians that "the time for Christian consciences to manifest themselves has come" and Cardinal Siri stated that it was mortal sin to vote for "lists and candidates who refuse to promise to respect God's rights as well as those of the Church and the citizens." (Ginsborg 154, 1989)

9. The term Zhdanovism takes its name from Andrei Zhdanov, a Soviet Central Committee Secretary who, in 1946, launched a campaign against any intellectual—including poets and novelists—whose works refused to conform to the Party lines. In Italy, the term was used to refer negatively to any censorship by the orthodox left-wing intelligentsia and the direction of the Party. Significantly, the first issue of *Frigidaire* (see

chapter 2), the comics magazine that in the early '80s signaled the defeat of the cultural cold-war climate, included an article and unpublished poems by Anna Akhmatova, one of the first victims of Soviet Zhdanovism.

10. When *Barbarella* finally reappeared in the pages of *Linus* in 1967, the editors—worried about their readers' reactions—cautiously used white-out to cover the heroine's exposed nipples. Censorship was still a two-way street in Italy.

11. The Italian *fumetti neri* and *vietati* also had great success in France and most of them were faithfully reprinted (with a slight delay) by the publisher Elvifrance.

12. "In simple terms the story is the *what* in a narrative that is depicted, discourse the *how*." (Chatman 19)

13. In the kaleidoscope of references that constitute one of the many discursive strategies of *The Hermetic Garage* (including cult science fiction author Michael Moorcock, Golden-Age American comics, Zen philosophy, French turn-of-the-century popular culture), Moebius goes as far as quoting his own '60s drawing style for the popular French character Blueberry by abruptly dropping his character in a western setting. An Italian artist who adopted Moebius's eclectic strategies and made them his own was Andrea Pazienza—one of the leading artists of Italian new adult comics.

14. The title, *the adventurist*, sarcastically referred both to a term used by the orthodox supporters of the Communist Party to label comrades who would ideologically stray from the directives of the party, and to the popular comic book magazine of the '30s, *L'Avventuroso*.

CHAPTER TWO

1. One year later, Andrea Valcarenghi, editor-in-chief of *Re Nudo*, reconsidering the event, wrote: "*Re Nudo* in particular needs to acknowledge some of its mistakes because, in this context of extreme social and cultural poverty, it thought it possible to gather together thousands of extremely diverse situations, imagining a possible aggregation while divisions were at the root, at a neighbourhood level." (in Bertante 164)

2. The 1973 strike at the Mirafiori (a factory in Turin belonging to the FIAT group) was the first example of autonomous organization of factory workers. Not only had the workers acted independently from the Communist Party, the unions, or the extra parliamentary groups, but it was the first hint of that refusal of work as an implicit value that will later define the youth Movement of '77. The Mirafiori strike officially marks the beginning of the independent movement of *autonomia* (autonomous action).

3. Potere Operaio was one of the most important extreme left-wing groups of the '68 period. When the group dissolved in 1973, some of its members joined the ranks of Autonomia Operaia and some the terrorist group Brigate Rosse. Among Potere Operaio's militants were Oreste Scalzone, Franco Piperno, and Toni Negri. The latter is a well-known socio-political expert in the United States due to the success of his study on late-capitalism, *Empire* (2000).

4. Toni Negri wrote, rather prophetically in 1974: "The extra-parliamentary groups are quickly dissolving, the only outcome seems to indicate a reconciliation with the institutions or, on the opposite, an individual determination towards terrorism. Smaller independent groups are formed, a mobile, unstable, and potentially dangerous growth unable to point to unified political solutions." (Balestrini 437)

5. The protests were originally caused by a reform proposal advanced by the Education Minister Franco Maria Malfatti. The reform included a norm prohibiting students to take more than one course on the same subject, thereby cancelling the liberty of choosing one's own curriculum—one of the hard-earned conquests of the '68 protests. The students also saw this proposal as the first step toward harsher counter-reformation measures.

6. Berlinguer was quoting Alessandro Manzoni's historical novel *I promessi sposi*. In seventeenth century Italy it was popular belief that the plague was intentionally spread by a group of men by means of an infected ointment, the *untori*. By its Manzonian reference, Berlinguer was ridiculing the protesters and belittling the importance and impact of the Movement.

7. On the 5th of July 1977 a group of French intellectuals including Sartre, Foucault, Guattari, Deleuze, and Barthes had sent an open letter to the journal *Lotta Continua* denouncing the political dangers of the *compromesso storico* and the harshness of police repression following the student protests: "We want to draw attention on the serious events occurring in Italy and in particular on the repression that is targeting militant factory workers and dissident intellectuals fighting against the *historic compromise* (. . .) Against the politics of austerity and sacrifice dictated by the government they replied with the occupation of the universities, mass demonstrations, wildcat strikes, sabotage and absenteeism in the factories, using all the ferocious irony and creativity of those who, cast out by the power of the institutions, have nothing to lose." (Balestrini 613)

8. *Work less, work more slowly* also became a popular song for the Movement that was often played in the independent radios of the time—at Radio Alice it signalled the beginning of morning broadcasting—and was also released commercially by a cultural association spawned by the newspaper *Lotta Continua* in 1974. The lyrics of the song invited its listeners to: "Work slowly without too much effort/who works fast hurts himself and winds up in an hospital/there's no room nowadays in hospitals and you could easily die/Work slowly, there's no price on health so slow down/pause pause slow rhythm/ Step out of the machine, live in slow motion." Enzo del Re, the author of the song, later worked with Nobel Prize winner Dario Fo, and his name has resurfaced with a recent movie on Radio Alice and the events of '77 bearing the same name of his notorious song: Guido Chiesa's *Lavorare con lentezza* (2004).

9. The stylistic element is rather diverse. Talking about a strike that happened during the spring, they say "April is the cruellest month." The enemy is attacked with a: "Toi, hypocrite lecteur, mon semblable, mon frère." Quotes used by Radio Alice do not hesitate to mix DeSade, Mayakovsky, Mandrake (the comic book magician), Artaud, and the hero Guattareuze (referring to the authors of the *Anti-Edipo*, Deleuze and Guattari)." (Eco, *Corriere della Sera* February 14, 1977)

10. Eco talked about it for the first time during a conference on the theory of mass media in 1965 in Perugia: "Instead of modifying the messages or controlling the sources of broadcasting, one could alter the communicative process acting instead on the circumstances in which the message will be received." (Gruber 141)

11. The white-collar worker Fantozzi is a popular Italian movie character. After the success of the first movie, actor Paolo Villaggio played the humble cubicle-dwelling, but potentially rebellious Fantozzi in six more features and many of the character's verbal idiosyncrasies and signature expressions have since become part of the Italians' own vocabulary.

12. The practice of *autoriduzione* (the reduction of the price of a restaurant check or the admission to a theatre or cinema imposed by the patrons themselves) was initiated in Bologna by Diego Benecchi, law student and founder of the *Gruppo Jaquerie*. "The fashion of *autoriduzione* spread fast, soon becoming a miniature mass phenomenon. Some business owners gave up after a while and admission to movie theatres became free for students, seniors, and the unemployed." (Vecchio, 75) By 1977, the movement had expanded *autoriduzione* to bookstores and supermarkets.

13. It is worth noting that Gaznevada originally belonged to the collective group Traumfabrik that, like a miniature version of Warhol's Factory, consisted of musicians, painters, and comic book artists. Traumfabrik was founded by Filippo Scòzzari, and the group also included cartoonist Andrea Pazienza.

14. "The interrelation between the language of music and that of comics is for me extremely stimulating; the project of providing a soundtrack for the magazine (*Frigidaire*), even though it presents many practical difficulties, has not yet been abandoned." (Tamburini, http://web.tiscali.it, 2000) *Frigidaire* would in fact present many instances of such interdependency: Roberto Antoni's column of album covers reviews, Tamburini's music reviews, contemporary composer Sylvano Bussotti's introductory essay to Tamburini's first comic book album, Carpinteri's comic book story "Rumble Mumble," which was intended to be read while listening to the Bologna band Stupid Set's song of the same name, and finally an issue with a seven-inch providing a soundtrack for the comics of the magazine.

15. This particular issue, the first to be regularly distributed in newspaper stands, sported four different covers, one by each of the *Cannibale* artists at that time, and could be read starting from the front, back (turning it upside down), or center.

16. Autonomia Operaia was a political group toward which many exponents of the autonomist area gravitated. Not a party or an extra-parliamentary group, but a loose structure encompassing many different orientations, Autonomia Operaia was defined by two distinct and often clashing components: the Marxist-Leninist one, indebted to the experience of post-'68 groups such as Potere Operaio; and the spontaneous anarchist one, represented by the student Movement. Toni Negri, Oreste Scalzone, Franco Piperno, and Bifo (Franco Berardi) were all intellectuals at one time tied to Autonomia Operaia. The group, whose activity peaked during the '77 protests, disbanded in 1978 as a result of both the split between the Marxist-Leninist activists and the student Movement—and the harsh police repression following Aldo Moro's killing.

17. Sabin, 94

18. Quite revealing on this subject is the banning of the strip *Dick Tracy* that was requested and obtained by *Alter Linus* readers in 1978 after unjustly accusing Chester Gould's character of crypto-Fascism and racism. The average reader of *Alter Linus*, extremely conscious of ideologies but superficial and manichiest when decoding them, belonged clearly to an old generation far removed from the ideal readership of *Cannibale* or *Il Male*.

19. In July 1976 an explosion at the Swiss-owned Icmesa factory (producing pesticides and defoliants) located close to the small northern town of Seveso caused the release of dioxine gas, a chemical linked to birth defects. The citizens were only notified of the accident two days later. On this occasion the Democratic Christian government led by Andreotti was forced to pass a law that allowed therapeutic abortion for the women of

Seveso. This was an important step towards the legalization of abortion two years later and represented one of the most clamorous defeats for the Christian Democrats.

20. *Il Male* reached a circulation of 120,000 copies per week after a fake conference in which a Pope impersonator spoke from the balcony of the office of *Il Male*. This final *fake* cost Sparagna a week of prison in solitary confinement.

CHAPTER THREE

1. Pazienza, who was supposed to graduate in semiotics under the direction of Umberto Eco, never completed his B.A. He did however get a start in his publishing career by introducing himself to the editorial board of *Alter* with a forged recommendation letter supposedly written by Eco himself.   •

2. Heroin had been present in Italy since the '60s, although its use was then limited and confined to the upper classes. The late '70s witnessed a sudden and dramatic increase in its use and availability. Although it is necessary to dismiss the improbable conspiracy theories that point to a direct responsibility of the government in the matter, the coincidence between "hot zones" of activism and political dissent (Bologna, Milano) and availability of the drug are certainly striking. Filippo Scòzzari, resident of Bologna during those years, witnessed firsthand the fast spread of the drug among his friends and fellow cartoonists: "I am still stupefied by the blindness of those who were in charge, the administration of the city of Bologna. You are the king of your city and programmer X decided to flood you with heroin. How could you not notice? How could you not take any action? There is no excuse. Clear symptoms were already coming from other parts of Italy: Milan, for example, where the problem had already taken a turn for the worse. One only had to read *Re Nudo* on whose pages the issue was constantly discussed and documented; read it, study it, and get ready. The administration didn't raise a finger. As a result, nowadays Bologna is a dead city and continues to enjoy attention way beyond its real merits." (Scòzzari 2002, conversation with the author)

3. See *Chapter Two*.

4. Although there are many theoretical studies dealing with modal narrative theory, Northrope Frye's *Anatomy of Criticism* being the one most often referred to, I chose to employ Scholes's formulation for its clarity, precision, and exhaustiveness.

5. Military service was obligatory in Italy until the late '90s. College students could postpone service provided they passed a yearly quota of exams.

6. Pazienza was extremely fond of linguistic *calembours*, which he would regularly employ, applying them also to his own name. These are disseminated through his entire output, among the many: "Andrei in Vacanza" (I would go on holiday) for Andrea Pazienza, and the bittersweet "Pompeo, lo stinco più stanco," a double entendre between the Italian expression "stinco di santo" (a saintly, virtuose, individual) and *the most spent person of all*.

7. It would be useful here to refer to Gadda's formulation of "combinatory reality" ("Manzoni diviso in tre dal bisturi di Moravia" in Isella, Dante, ed. *Il tempo e le opere*. Milano: Adelphi, 1982, p. 32), rather than to an equivocal notion of realism, because it is ultimately the combination of the internal relationships of a text which constitute its particular reality.

8. According to Jameson, *pastiche* is a typically postmodern mode. Pastiche, unlike satire, posits itself in a neutral rather than antagonistic relationship with its materials, materials with which the text does not any longer entertain any kind of "historical" relationship (Jameson 16–19). The proof, in the case of Scòzzari's adaptation, is that irony is not addressed toward the original source as belonging to a specific category (novel, noir, American fiction) or for purporting any specific ideology, but rather toward the text itself in its individuality.

9. "I saw the movie, broadcast by a private TV station, three or four years after having published my comic adaptation. It was terribly boring. If one were to put it into antagonistic terms, I easily won. First of all, between the movie and my version there had been forty years of development in narrative techniques. Also, I did not kneel down in the presence of Chandler, I fought with him and I think this attitude helped to modernize a pretty weak story." (Scòzzari 2002, conversation with the author)

10. In the first episodes, the character was called Rank Xerox after a photocopy machine brand name; the name was changed to Ranxerox after its namesake company threatened to sue its creators.

11. The centrality of these *topoi* in Calvino's later fictional works are underlined by Remo Ceserani, in his study on Italian literary postmodern, *Raccontare il postmoderno*.

12. Among the many authors forged by Brolli are: Ernest Hemingway, Philip K. Dick, Stephen King, Kurt Vonnegut, Jr., Boris Vian, William Gibson, Ian McEwan, and J. G. Ballard.

CONCLUSIONS

1. Following the dramatic increase in the cost of paper in 1982, the state instituted a reimbursement aimed at "cultural" publications to be paid within four years. *Frigidaire*, like other monthlies, had accumulated many debts the magazine hoped to repay with the reimbursement. By March 1986, it became known that the Commissione Editoria (the state commission which was supposed to award the reimbursements), chaired by Giuliano Amato, member of Bettino Craxi's Socialist Party (a frequent target of Vincenzo Sparagna's caustic editorials for *Frigidaire*), had denied *Frigidaire* the status of "cultural" publication and hence refused to award the 600 million Liras the magazine was expecting to receive. With this criminal decision against *Frigidaire*, Italian comic artists, which were becoming the leading force in the European scene, were reduced to starving in their own country. The most important and revolutionary cultural magazine in Italy was artificially brought to its knees by the voting of a commission whose responsibility, later, nobody acknowledged: "'I didn't understand,' 'I wasn't there,' 'I didn't know,' 'I didn't vote because I was the chair,' that's how Amato justified himself." (Sparagna 2009, 162) From this point on, *Frigidaire*, unable to pay its contributors, lost many of its trademark artists, and was forced to depend on *pro bono* contributions. Pazienza, Liberatore, and Mattioli all fled to other publications.

2. In 1987 William Scobe commented from the pages of the *Observer*: "Italy finally has become, in 1987, one of Europe's greatest success stories. Suddenly, this is a land of upward mobility, of vital computerized industry, bustling young business managers and

slick middle-aged tycoons who have abjured their sixties ideals in the sacred cause of profit. Class war is passé." ("La dolce Italia," 15 November, 1987.)

3. The exact figures for the year 1978 are: 2,275 private radio stations in Italy versus 8,240 in the United States; and 503 private TV channels in Italy versus 984 in the U.S. (Gruber 54)

Bibliography

Antoni, Roberto. *Le stagioni del rock demenziale*. Milano: Feltrinelli, 1981.

Balestrini, Nanni, and Paolo Moroni. *L'orda d'oro, 1968–1977. La grande ondata rivoluzionaria e creativa, politica ed esistenziale*. Milano: Feltrinelli, 1997.

Barbieri, Daniele. *Valvoforme e Valvocolori*. Milano: Idea Books, 1990.

———. *Breve storia della letteratura a fumetti*. Roma: Carocci, 2009.

Barilli, Renato. *Prima e dopo il 2000, la ricerca artistica 1970–2005*. Milano: Feltrinelli, 2006.

Baudrillard, Jean. *Seduction*. New York: Palgrave Macmillan, 1991.

Berardi, Franco, and Veronica Bridi, eds. *1977, l'anno in cui il futuro incominciò*. Roma: Fandango, 2002.

Bertante, Alessandro. *Re Nudo, underground e rivoluzione nelle pagine di una rivista*. Rimini: NdA Press, 2005.

Bianchi, Sergio, and Lanfranco Caminiti, eds. *'77, la rivoluzione che viene*. Roma: DeriveApprodi, 2007.

Bonito Oliva, Achille. *The Italian Trans-avantgarde*. Milano: Politi, 1981.

———. *Trans-avantgarde international*. Milano: Politi, 1982.

Boschi, Luca. *Frigo, valvole e balloons, viaggio in vent'anni di fumetto italiano d'autore*. Roma: Theoria, 1997.

———. *Irripetibili, Le grandi stagioni del fumetto italiano*. Roma: Coniglio, 2007.

Brancato, Sergio. *Fumetti, guida ai comics nel sistema dei media*. Roma: Datanews, 1994.

Calabrese, Omar. "L'eterno rinnovamento del volgare." *Andrea Pazienza*. Pazienza, Marina, and Mauro Paganelli. Montepulciano: Il Grifo, 1991.

Carpinteri, Giorgio. *Flirt*. Roma: Primo Carnera, 1982.

Ceserani, Remo. *Raccontare il postmoderno*. Torino: Bollati Boringhieri, 2006.

Chatman, Seymour. *Story and Discourse, Narrative Structure in Fiction and Film*. London: Cornell University Press, 1980.

Echaurren, Pablo. *Parole ribelli, i fogli del movimento del '77*. Roma: Stampa Alternativa, 1997.

Eco, Umberto. *The Name of the Rose*. Orlando: Harvest, 1994.

El Kohlti, Heidi, and Sylvère Lotringer, Christian Marazzi, ed. *Autonomia: Post-political politics*. Cambridge: MIT Press, 2007.

Farina, Roberto. *I dolori del giovane Paz! Contributi alla biografia negata di Andrea Pazienza*. Roma: Coniglio, 2005.

Ghedini, Rudi. *Andrea Pazienza. i segni di una resa invincibile*. Torino: Bradipo Libri, 2005.

Ginsborg, Paul. *L' Italia del tempo presente, Famiglia, società civile, Stato, 1980–1996*. Torino: Einaudi, 1988.

———. *Storia d'Italia dal dopoguerra a oggi, società e politica, 1943–1988*. Torino: Einaudi, 1989.

Giubilei, Franco. *Le donne, i cavalieri, l'arme, la roba, storia e storie di Andrea Pazienza.* Roma: Edizioni BD, 2006.

Gruber, Klemens. *L'avanguardia inaudita, comunicazione e strategia nei movimenti degli anni Settanta.* Milano: Costa & Nolan, 1997.

Hoesterey, Ingeborg. *Pastiche: Cultural Memory in Art, Film, Literature.* Bloomington: Indiana University Press, 2001.

Jameson, Frederic. *Postmodernism, or, the Cultural Logic of Late-Capitalism.* Durham: Duke University Press, 1991.

Mattioli, Massimo. *Joe Galaxy e le perfide lucertole di Callisto IV.* Roma: Primo Carnera, 1982.

———. *Squeak the Mouse.* Roma: Primo Carnera, 1986.

Mollica, Vincenzo. *Milo Manara/Andrea Pazienza.* Montepulciano: Editori del Grifo, 1982.

Mordente, Michele, ed. *Stefano Tamburini, banana meccanica.* Roma: Coniglio, 2006.

———. *Una matita a serramanico, omaggio a Stefano Tamburini.* Milano: Stampa Alternativa, 1997.

Origa, Graziano, ed. *Vietato ai minori, Vamp e vampire: Jacula, Zora, Sukia e Yra.* Milano: Rizzoli, 2007.

Paganelli, Mauro, Pazienza Comandini, Marina, ed. *Andrea Pazienza.* Montepulciano: Editori del Grifo, 1991.

Pazienza, Andrea. *Aficionados.* Roma: Primo Carnera, 1981.

———. *Andrea Pazienza.* Città di Castello: Il Male, 1981.

———. *Cose d'A.Paz.* Roma: Primo Carnera, 1988.

———. *Le straordinarie avventure di Pentothal.* Milano: Milano Libri, 1982.

———. *Perchè Pippo sembra uno sballato.* Roma: Primo Carnera, 1983.

———. *Pertini.* Roma: Primo Carnera, 1983.

———. *Pompeo.* Montepulciano, Del Grifo, 1987.

———. *The Great.* Roma: Primo Carnera, 1988.

———. *Tormenta.* Milano: Milano Libri, 1985.

———. *Zanardi.* Roma: Primo Carnera, 1983.

———. *Zanardi e altre storie.* Roma: Comic Art, 1988.

Piselli, Stefano, and Riccardo Morocchi. *Esotika Erotika Psicotika kaleidoscopic sexy Italia 1964–1973.* Firenze: Glittering Images, 2000.

Rossi, Sergio. *Maledette vi amerò, le grandi eroine del fumetto erotico italiano.* Milano: Neri Pozza, 2007.

Sabin, Roger. *Comics, Comix & Graphic Novels, a History of Comic Art.* New York: Phaidon Press, 2001.

Scholes, Robert. *Structuralism in Literature.* New Haven: Yale University Press, 1974.

Scòzzari, Filippo. *Altri cieli.* Roma: Primo Carnera, 1989.

———. *Donne.* Roma: Primo Carnera, 1986.

———. *Dottor Jack.* Roma: Primo Carnera, 1983.

———. *Fango e ossigeno.* Roma: Primo Carnera, 1988.

———. *Figate.* Milano: Mare-Nero, 1999.

———. *La Dalia azzurra.* Roma: Primo Carnera, 1982.

———. *Memorie dell'arte bimba.* Roma: Coniglio, 2008.

———. *Prima pagare poi ricordare, da Cannibale a Frigidaire, storia di un manipolo di ragazzi geniali.* Roma: Castelvecchi, 1998.

———. *Primo Carnera*. Roma: Primo Carnera, 1982.

———. *Suor Dentona e altre battaglie*. Roma: Primo Carnera, 1989.

———. *XXXX! Racconti porni*. Roma: Castelvecchi, 1997.

Sparagna, Vincenzo. *Frigidaire, l'incredibile storia e le sorprendenti avventure della più rivoluzionaria rivista d'arte del mondo*. Milano: Rizzoli, 2008.

Tamburini, Stefano, and Tanino Liberatore. *Ranxerox*. Roma: Primo Carnera, 1981.

———. *Tenere Violenze, storie di sesso, d'amore, d'orrore*. Roma: Primo Carnera, 1988.

Varnedoe, Kirk, and Adam Gopnik. *High and Low, Modern Art and Popular Culture*. New York: Museum of Modern Art, 1990.

Vecchio, Concetto. *Ali di piombo, il 1977 trent'anni dopo*. Milano: Rizzoli, 2007.

Vincino. *Il Male, 1978–1982, i cinque anni che cambiarono la satira*. Milano: Rizzoli, 2007.

VV.AA. *Bologna marzo 1977 . . . fatti nostri . . .* Rimini: NdA Press, 2007.

MAGAZINES

Alterlinus. Milano: Rizzoli, 1974–1986.

Cannibale. Roma: Il Male, 1977–1979.

Comic Art. Milano, 1984–1999.

Dolce Vita. Milano, 1986–1988.

Eureka. Milano: Editoriale Corno, 1968–1984.

Frigidaire. Roma: Primo Carnera, 1980–

Il Mago. Milano: Mondadori, 1972–1981.

Il Male. Roma, 1978–1982.

Linus. Milano: Rizzoli, 1965–

Re Nudo. Milano, 1968–1976.

Index

Breinigsville, PA USA
12 November 2010
249271BV00002B/1/P